GRAFFITI

GRAFFITI
LEARNING TO SEE THE ART IN OURSELVES

ERIN DAVIS

MOODY PUBLISHERS
CHICAGO

Library of Congress Cataloging-in-Publication Data

Davis, Erin, 1980-
Graffiti : learning to see the art in ourselves / by Erin Davis.
   p. cm.
Includes bibliographical references.
ISBN 978-0-8024-4585-8
   1. Self-esteem--Religious aspects--Christianity. 2. Self-acceptance--Religious aspects--Christianity. 3. Beauty, Personal. I. Title.
   BV4598.24.D38 2008
   248.8'33--dc22
                  2008005515

To Jason, who has always seen my beauty.

CONTENTS

When people ask me what this book is about, I am thrilled to explain that it is about exploring our beauty through the filter of God's Word.

When they ask me what the title is, and I respond by telling them that it's *Graffiti*, they often look perplexed.

"Graffiti?" they ask. "What does that have to do with beauty?"

Over the years, I have come to admire graffiti as a beautiful art form. I am intrigued by the shapes and colors painted on train cars and bridges. I often marvel at the uniqueness of each drawing. The world finds it hard to look past the vandalism—and I am certainly not advocating defaming public property—but while most people don't recognize the appeal of art made with a can of spray paint instead of a brush, I have come to realize that true beauty is often found in the places where the world does not recognize worth.

Our beauty is like this. The world expects us to ascribe to a version of beauty that is common and predictable and easily framed by their standards. Magazines and billboards offer us a version of beauty that focuses on perfection, and we begin to question our own worth because we can't measure up.

I am not the first author to recognize that generations of young women have struggled to embrace their God-given worth and are questioning their inherent beauty. So you may be wondering, "Why *Graffiti*? Why pick up this book?" My search for freedom from the bondage of self-doubt took off when I started to look at God's Word for answers.

What I found was that from Genesis to Revelation God's Word offers specific assurances of our value, worth, and beauty. The answer to my longing to be beautiful wasn't as simple as "God loves me just the way I am," but instead, the answers were found in a series of complex truths that God lovingly offers through Scripture.

In this book, we will also take a hard look at the consequences of failing to see our beauty. We'll learn why what we think affects how we act by exploring a theory on broken windows, and we'll study our responsibility in choosing to believe God's Word instead of the misguided messages the world sends our way.

It is my prayer that you will find the freedom to stop striving for beauty based on worldly acceptance and find strength in comfort in the assurances offered to the created by the Creator.

WHAT I SEE IN THE MIRROR:
INSIGHT INTO THE HEART OF MY STRUGGLE

I kneeled on the floor of my tiny bathroom gasping for control. For the third time in a week, the urge to take drastic measures consumed me after my scale screamed numbers that made me cringe.

Intense conversations with my Savior had helped me avoid purging twice before, but this time the battle was too fierce, and I surrendered to my temptation as tears of frustration streamed down my face.

"How did I get to this place?" I whispered. "I thought I was past this."

That day in the bathroom and many other days like it stand out as monumental moments in my struggle to embrace my beauty. I whimpered those words early in 2003, a year when everything seemed to be going right. I was a new bride who had recently married the man of my dreams. We were gladly serving as youth pastors on staff at a welcoming church in a charming town. My career was taking off. I had many friends. I seemed to be in control. What could be wrong?

I knew the answer: me. I was wrong. Every time I looked in the mirror I knew that I was flawed, and my reflection confirmed that I was ugly, fat, and shameful.

On that day when I knelt on the floor after attempting to regain control of my beauty by doing whatever it took to control my weight, I heard lies being whispered that I had believed a thousand times before. Even though it had been nearly two years since I had acted out my eating disorder, I hadn't gone a single day since without thinking I had no value or worth or beauty to offer.

For as long as I can remember, the temptation to turn my eyes from the prize and toward my thighs—thighs that are too big and abs that aren't flat enough—has been a thorn in my flesh. At times it seems that I am being hunted, literally chased by an enemy who knows that an obsession with my physical body naturally leads to an unraveling of my focus on all that God has for me.

I have had many, many moments of struggle in the area of beauty. These moments are my most intimate secrets, the deepest places of my heart. It would be easier not to admit these weaknesses to you. I would prefer for you to think that I have it all together. But I feel compelled to give you a glimpse into the heart of my struggle.

Why? Because I know you struggle too. I am sure of it. I am not the only girl to feel this way. I have learned this lesson as part of my healing. As the Lord began to call me out of the pit of self-doubt, He asked me to share my heart with others. I began, reluctantly at first, I admit, to travel the country to talk with girls just like you. I have heard you comment about your thighs and bellies. I see you watch each other and compare every curve. I have stood by and watched as the Enemy has whispered the same lies into your life that he spent years whispering into mine. "You are fat," he says. "You are ugly." "Other girls are more beautiful than you." "There is something wrong with you." "You don't have value."

And so we wonder: Are we flawed, are we a mistake . . . could we be beautiful?

The answers to these questions are the keys to our freedom. But we must seek them out. God's Word is rich with words of affirmation of our beauty and worth, but we must seek His truth in order to counteract the lies that are so tightly wrapped around our hearts. Maybe these lies have never led you to take the actions I have taken to be beautiful. But this is not a book about actions; it is an exploration of your heart. If you've ever doubted your beauty and worth, you have heard a lie. Freedom from the lie—for you and for me—is important, and yes, you can find it!

We fight side by side in a battle with a slippery snake. I know from experience that this is a battle not easily won. But I also know that victory comes when you turn your eyes upon Jesus.

You are not the only one who has heard or seen the lie. You are not the only one who doesn't like what she sees in the mirror. You certainly aren't the only one to question your own beauty.

I want you to know that there *is* a mirror that does not mock. There *is* a place where we can look and be told that we are beautiful, lovely, treasured. That mirror is Christ, and believe it or not, He has dedicated much of His Word to exploring your beauty and affirming your worth.

What about You?

It is my deep desire for this book to become a conversation—both a conversation between you and me as we both examine our beauty under the microscope of God's Word, and also a conversation between you and Christ, the author of your beauty. But conversations require two-way communication. So at the end of each chapter, there is space for you to write about your own experiences and reactions. It might take some effort. For many of us, these issues of ourselves and our beauty are so deeply ingrained that it is difficult to sift through them and see what exactly our feelings are and where they have come from. You'll see questions to guide you, but feel free to write about what's on your heart. I am praying for the Holy Spirit to minister mightily to you through these pages.

Start by writing a letter to God. Tell Him where you are in your struggle to embrace your own beauty. Ask Him to begin to help you identify lies that you have believed in this area of your life, and be open to His truth in these areas. Tell Him that you are ready to have a conversation about your beauty, and invite

Him to guide the direction of the communication. I promise you that the words of love He has to offer will surprise you and affirm you in ways you never thought possible.

So will you come along with me on a journey? Will you join me as we examine together what Christ has to say about your beauty? Do you have the courage to look deep into your own heart as I continue to reveal the deepest parts of mine? Let's take the journey together. I am praying that you will walk away with a renewed sense of worth and the ability to see that your beauty is God-given and that you truly are His masterpiece.

2

THE HISTORY OF BEAUTY:
WHO CAN KEEP UP?

Let's imagine that you are getting ready for a dance. All of your friends are going to be there. Your date is really cute and he will be arriving to pick you up in a horse-drawn carriage in just a few hours (very Prince Charming–like!). Your dress is gorgeous—you feel like a princess in it! You have been waiting for this night for weeks.

You've spent hours before your date arrives getting ready. You've already had a long bath in donkey's milk to make your skin soft and fresh. You've plucked your eyebrows into a fashionable narrow arch. You've picked out the perfect curly red wig to match your bright red lips and cheeks. You know that every other beautiful girl there will have skin the color of alabaster, so you apply your own white foundation, a concoction made of white lead and vinegar. Since transparent skin is all the rage, you paint on false veins and you brighten your eyes with drops made from belladonna plants. It's true that this plant is toxic, but hey, it's necessary to give your eyes sparkle.

Does this sound like a fashion nightmare? Is it hard to imagine finding pale, almost sickly, skin more attractive than the healthy look we sun worshipers go for?

Can you imagine putting toxins in your eyes to make them sparkle, or *painting on veins* to make your skin appear transparent? Sounds crazy!

But if you were a young lady living in the days of Queen Elizabeth I, these would be normal beauty standards. Instead of pining for the thin bodies, tan skin, and gorgeous long hair of today's popular culture icons, you would have spent your time wishing that you could achieve the look of Queen Elizabeth herself. She was known throughout the land as the ultimate standard of beauty. She boasted very pale skin, wore a red wig, her lips were the brightest red, and she had an extremely high hairline that she achieved by—are you ready?—plucking. Ouch![1]

Queen Elizabeth wasn't the only woman whose standard of beauty seems far-fetched to us. Cleopatra's lipsticks were made from finely crushed beetles mixed with ant eggs.[2] Several Egyptian queens wore false beards to important ceremonies.[3] Closer to our time, during the Second World War, women tanned their legs with browning gravy or strong tea because, due to rationing, no silk stockings were available.[4]

A study of the history of beauty reads more to us like a *Fear Factor* cookbook than a fashion magazine! One culture's idea of a beautiful woman is another era's candidate for a makeover. But no matter in what age we live, we as women have struggled with or been determined to fit into the beauty mold of the time.

Great Lengths

In fact, women have always gone to great lengths to feel beautiful. We have worked hard to measure up for centuries.

That alabaster skin I mentioned earlier was considered an essential item for the fashionable woman four hundred years ago, but it also caused a variety of skin problems. Some beauty writers at the time discouraged this practice, pointing out that it made skin appear grey and shriveled. Even worse, the foundation was responsible for numerous physical problems and even resulted in some cases of muscle paralysis and untimely death.[5]

During the Renaissance, wealthy Italian women wore a popular face powder made of arsenic. They were encouraged to apply the powder when their husbands were around. In a gruesome twist to this odd trend, the creator of the powder was later executed after as many as six hundred husbands died from exposure to the poison.[6]

In ancient China, small feet were considered beautiful. So, from age six on, young Chinese girls' feet were bound to keep them from growing. A perfectly bound foot would only be about three inches long. That standard of beauty kept women from walking, running, and dancing.[7]

Have you ever heard of the Padung tribe of Burma? I bet you've heard of their beauty standards. They are famous for considering long necks beautiful and for taking extreme measures to achieve that look. They use neck rings to stretch the necks of the women of their tribe to as long as fifteen inches, causing major deformities.

These beauty standards sound bizarre. It is hard to imagine that women have worked hard for white skin, tiny, useless feet, and giraffe-like necks, or that men have found those traits endearing. Even stranger when you think about it is the fact that women throughout history have felt insecure or questioned their own worth because they couldn't achieve the standard of beauty that was currently in vogue . . . painted-on veins? Giraffe neck? Arsenic-laced powder?

But are we any different today? Our society, like every society throughout the ages, is obsessed with beauty and has invented a slew of new ways to obtain beauty at any cost. From plastic surgery to Botox to obsession resulting in eating disorders, it's not hard to imagine what the history books will tell about the great lengths we are willing to go to so we can meet the current beauty ideal.

Weighing In . . . It's All Relative

For most of us, beauty isn't about hair, makeup, and fashion nearly as much as it is about our bodies. If you are like me, the words *beautiful* and *thin* are synonyms. How many times have you told yourself, "If I could just lose ten pounds, then I would be beautiful," or "If I were as thin as she is, then I would be beautiful"?

For many of us, and for women throughout the ages, our struggle to achieve the weight standards of our society causes untold grief and frustration.

It is certainly true that in our culture weight is a key beauty issue. The ultra-thin ideals of beauty that we see in magazines, movies, and television are the models of beauty that we feel pressured to become. Here's proof:

- According to a recent study, over half of the females between the ages of 18 and 25 would prefer to be run over by a truck than to be fat. Two thirds of women in that age group would choose to be mean or stupid rather than fat.[8]

- The number one wish for females 11 to 17 is to lose weight.[9]

- According to one study, 20 percent of *underweight* adolescent girls actively diet.[10] 91 percent of women recently surveyed on a college campus had attempted to control their weight through dieting; 22 percent dieted "often" or "always."

- 40 percent of newly identified cases of anorexia are in girls 15 to 19.

- There has been a rise in incidence of anorexia in 15- to19-year-olds every year since 1930.[11]

My weight has been a core issue in my life since junior high. My thoughts are constantly ruled by wishes to be thin and by frustration over my lack of willpower to get that way. As much as I don't like to admit it, I find myself thinking about my weight more than I think about my family, my friends, or my Savior.

I wonder if the same is true for you. Do you fit into these statistics somewhere? Maybe you are unhappy with your body. Maybe you are among the 91 percent of us who have dieted or the 22 percent of us who are almost always dieting.

Or maybe you are among the growing number of girls who are so consumed by today's beauty standards that eating has become a luxury that you can't afford.

I understand! I can identify with nearly every negative body image statistic ever written. And we have plenty of company with women throughout history. As we've seen, a society's perception of the ideal female body type can change as quickly as the hemline, but the struggle to measure up is always with us.

In the 1890s, curves were in (too bad I didn't live then!). So women who were naturally thin put on false thighs and hips to make themselves appear fuller. Can you imagine padding your hips and thighs to feel more beautiful?

By the 1920s curves were out and boyish figures were in. Women worked for super-thin bodies. In contrast to our society today, shapely chests and backsides were considered unattractive.

Then the pendulum swung back in the 1950s when Marilyn Monroe's size-14 body was considered ideal. And two decades later, women longed for the model Twiggy's 5'-7" 91-pound body.

Here's the scoop: Every society has an ideal in weight that's considered attractive, and most of us will never achieve the ideal. So how do we deal with this reality?

Cultivating Lasting Beauty

In light of the evidence that what society considers beautiful is constantly changing—what's a girl to do? How about if we spend our time working on beauty that lasts? God's Word offers us some clues for how to obtain beauty that transcends the constantly changing trends of the world.

Peter writes, "Your beauty should not come from outward adornment, such as braided hair and the wearing of gold jewelry and fine clothes. Instead, it should be that of your inner self, the unfading beauty of a gentle and quiet spirit, which is of great worth in God's sight" (1 Peter 3:3–4).

Does Peter have a problem with braids? Does he dislike gold jewelry? Is he saying that we can't wear cute clothes? No, that's not it. But he does seem to realize what a glance at the history of beauty easily reveals . . . any beauty obtained by something we can put on or take off our bodies is sure to fade. Sometimes braided hair is in style; sometimes it's not. Sometimes gold is the ultimate accent color. Sometimes it is "so last season." Sometimes a must-have outfit makes it to the bargain bin before I have the chance to buy it. Peter points out that something so temporary cannot be the source of true beauty.

But there *is* a source of true beauty.

Look again. Peter does mention a type of beauty that is unfading, one that lasts. Beauty that is not subject to whatever is considered hot at the moment—or who. He points out that lasting beauty comes from within, from a gentle and quiet spirit. And then he says the most amazing thing! He reminds us that not only does inner beauty last, but it is of great worth to God. Can you imagine anything more wonderful than developing a kind of beauty that the God of the universe treasures?

Paul offers valuable instruction in Philippians. Instead of focusing on the standards of this world, Paul encourages us to turn our attention toward things more eternal.

In Philippians 4:8 he writes, "Whatever is true, whatever is noble, whatever is right, whatever is pure, whatever is lovely, whatever is admirable—if anything is excellent or praise-worthy—think about such things."

I wonder if the beauty standards of this world could be considered true or noble. I wonder if something as flighty as the current ideal of the perfect weight could be considered pure or admirable. I wonder if the people we see in fashion magazines would be lovely without all of the wonders of makeup, lighting, and Photoshop.

When Audrey Hepburn, a timeless beauty icon, was asked to share her beauty tips she offered similar advice to Paul's by giving the words to the following poem:

For attractive lips, speak words of kindness.
For lovely eyes, seek out the good in people.
For a slim figure, share your food with the hungry.
For beautiful hair, let a child run his/her
fingers through it once a day.
For poise, walk with the knowledge
that you never walk alone.[12]

Beauty that doesn't depend on what we wear or weigh sounds like something attractive, doesn't it? Are you beginning to catch a glimpse of the freedom that can come when we start to chase godly beauty with the same fervor that we chase the beauty standards of this world? What about the beauty that can be found in that freedom?

I hope you're catching on, because no fashion model in the world can match the loveliness of a young woman who understands the true source of her beauty and decides to turn her eyes toward those things that are truly admirable, excellent, and worthy of praise.

♡ JOURNAL PROMPTS

1. What fashion trends have you participated in or that once appealed to you seem silly now?

2. If our culture's view of what is beautiful is constantly changing, how can we cultivate lasting beauty?

3. How do you develop inner beauty, especially a gentle and quiet spirit? What actions are necessary to develop these qualities?

3

WALKING ON BROKEN GLASS:
WHY WHAT YOU THINK AFFECTS HOW YOU LIVE

Let's take a walk. We'll head to a quiet neighborhood where the houses are attractive, the lawns are mowed, and the sidewalks are clean. We can take a deep breath of fresh air and enjoy listening to the sound of happy children playing. We'll talk about the comfortable homes that line both sides of the street and imagine together about the wonderful lives that are lived out within their walls.

I'll bet throwing rocks would be the furthest thing from our minds. I doubt that we'd be tempted to pick up stones and hurl them through the windows of neighborhood houses, especially the one with windows trimmed with beautifully painted shutters and flower boxes.

But what if we chose a different route? What if we walked through a neighborhood that was far less manicured and inviting? This second neighborhood has been neglected. The houses need paint. Many of their windows have been busted out. The sidewalks are cracked. Graffiti is everywhere. Because lawns have not been mowed, weeds have grown up, choking what grass remains.

Would we throw rocks here? Since most of the windows are already broken, wouldn't it be easy to pick up a stone and toss it through one of the few windows that remain? Would we be tempted to leave our trash on the ground, knowing that it would blend in well with the piles of litter that already cover the sidewalks? If we were ever going to experiment with graffiti, wouldn't this be the place to start? Who would notice? Who would care?

Criminologists have developed what they call the "broken windows theory" that answers these same questions. The theory asserts that a broken window or a littered sidewalk does no great harm to a neighborhood if promptly addressed. But if these things are left unattended, they send a signal that no one cares about that neighborhood, that it is a safe place to break things, to litter, to vandalize. Law enforcement officers and sociologists tend to agree that if a window in a building is broken and is left broken, the rest of the windows will soon be broken too.[1] Graffiti sends the message that an environment is uncontrolled and a place where damage can be done and no one cares. Trash on the sidewalk encourages passersby to add to the heap and not to worry about missing the trash can.

But what does this have to do with our beauty? When translated to our lives, and to our feelings about our identity and worth, the broken windows theory means that how we view ourselves matters. Many of us have become run-down neighborhoods. When we feel worthless, flawed, and broken, it makes it easier to behave in such a way that encourages others to throw stones toward our already hurting hearts.

Anna knows this all too well. She didn't believe what God's Word said about her worth, and she bought in to the beauty lies the world was telling her. Her sense of value cracked, and she unknowingly invited others to participate in the destruction process. Here's her story.

"For as long as I can remember, I've always had low self-esteem. I was always self-conscious and unfortunately it showed. I didn't want to stand out. I liked being invisible.

"Between eighth and ninth grade I started taking more notice of guys, so I lost the weight I thought was necessary. By the end of eighth grade signs of depression were already starting to show. I already knew that something wasn't right, but for a while I was able to hide the anger and disgust I felt toward myself.

"Then I got a boyfriend. I should have waited for a guy who was worth my time, but I still felt worthless and ugly. I wanted so desperately for someone to care for me in that way. So maybe even if I couldn't love myself, I could at least like myself."

Anna's boyfriend cheated on her, throwing another rock toward her cracked image of herself. She continued to seek validation from others and soon started dating another guy, but this time the consequences were more severe. She endured mental abuse, and her thoughts eventually turned to suicide. Hanging on to the edge of destruction, she heard God whisper about His love for her and His plan for her life. She sought help. Her wounds started to heal, but she soon repeated the cycle.

"He did abuse me some, both mentally and physically," Anna says about her next boyfriend. "When he got bored with me we'd break up so he could try out another girl he had lined up. For whatever reason it wouldn't work and he'd come back to me.

"No matter how far I had come with overcoming depression and suicidal thoughts, I held next to no value in myself and it showed."

Anna's failure to understand her worth eventually led to another destructive relationship that ended in rape. Nothing Anna did warranted the treatment she endured, but her failure to see her God-given worth became a foundational reason for her poor relationship choices. Without even knowing it, she sent out an invitation announcing that her life was a place where destruction was welcomed, that her heart was an area that was already so damaged that no one would notice if more wounds were added. The good news is that she is now on the long path toward healing and restoration.

Anna's story reminds me so much of my own. During the years when I most questioned my worth, I was prone to relationships that were destructive. Especially in my dating relationships, my picker-outer was simply broken. I tended to gravitate toward boys who would devalue me during that season of my life instead of looking for partners who treated me like God's temple. In my friendships, I chose to spend time with other girls who were needy and dependent. Instead of nurturing healthy friendships, I developed relationships with girls who were also self-destructive.

I have found that stories like my own and like Anna's are common. When we seek affirmation of our beauty from sources other than God and His Word, when we are confused about who we are, when we become self-conscious, our tendency is to fill those voids with attention from individuals who confirm that we lack worth.

Not everyone allows herself to be ensnared by abusive and unhealthy relationships, but many of us desperately seek confirmation of our beauty and worth from the men around us. This is the theme of Mary's story.

"It seems I can never measure up. Usually, when I am most unhappy with my physical body is when I am not in tune with God either. Why are girls much happier with a boyfriend? Maybe it's because we hear comments like 'you look nice today' more often. Who knows, but it seems that when I get a boyfriend, I tend to look to him in finding my beauty instead of the only One who can reveal my real beauty, God. I have struggled to try to turn my perspective toward God's view of beauty in my life."

The temptation to allow boys (or anyone else, for that matter) to define our worth is dangerous indeed. Even the most perfect boy will fall short if he becomes our source of security. That is because they are human, prone to mess up, guaranteed to have a bad day now and then, and sure to offer an unkind word at least every once in a while.

Jesus, on the other hand, is the same yesterday, today, and forever. His feelings for us do not waver. His loving countenance does not change. He consistently draws us to Himself and promises that He loves us, that He died for us, that He is preparing a place for us.

In fact, Jesus once spent time with a woman who knew a thing or two about throwing stones. Remember the adulterous woman? Let me remind you of Christ's kindness in the face of her brokenness.

John 7:53–8:11 tells a story of a woman whose life was broken indeed. She had been caught in the act of adultery, and the religious leaders of the time set out to make an example of her.

 Then each went to his own home. But Jesus went to the Mount of Olives. At dawn he appeared again in the temple courts, where all the people gathered around him, and he sat down to teach them. The teachers of the law and the Pharisees brought in a woman caught in adultery. They made her stand before the group and said to Jesus, "Teacher, this woman was caught in the act of adultery. In the Law Moses commanded us to stone such women. Now what do you say?" They were using this question as a trap, in order to have a basis for accusing him.

Can you imagine what this woman was feeling? She had been caught in the very act of adultery, and now she had been dragged in front of a crowd. The men who were with her were declaring her sin to everyone. She had nowhere to hide. There was no escape.

What is more, she had been stripped of her identity. No one cared about her name. The elements of her identity had been replaced by a label of "adulterer." It was all the world around her saw when they looked at her. The beauty that she had to offer the world was eclipsed by the narrow opinions of others.

What labels are you wearing? Do you fear that "ugly" is all that people see when they look at you? What about "fat" or "not good enough"? Do you wear the label of "shamed" or "lonely" or "sad"? Do you feel like your identity has been reduced to what you look like? That people cannot see beyond your face and body into the depths of your heart?

I bet the adulterous woman had felt that too. We don't know much about her, but we do know that she had made relationship choices that had brought her to the brink of destruction. She had sought solace in the arms of a man who was not her husband, and that relationship had left her life tattered.

But we get a glimpse into Christ's character when we examine His response.

 But Jesus bent down and started to write on the ground with his finger. When they kept on questioning him, he straightened up and said to them, "If any one of you is without sin, let him be the first to throw a stone at her." Again he stooped down and wrote on the ground.

At this, those who heard began to go away one at a time, the older ones first, until only Jesus was left, with the woman still standing there. Jesus straightened up and asked her, "Woman, where are they? Has no one condemned you?"

"No one, sir," she said.

"Then neither do I condemn you," Jesus declared. "Go now and leave your life of sin."

Jesus saw more than an adulterer. He didn't ignore her sin, but He looked beyond it, knowing that she had more to offer than this mistake. He protected her from the stones that others wanted to throw at her, and most important, He acted lovingly toward her. He does the same for us.

Christ is able to put a hedge of protection around our hearts that will keep us safe from those who want to throw stones. He is able to clean up our lives and mend up the broken places. He acts lovingly toward us, not because He doesn't see our flaws, but because He cares for us anyway. If He were to label us, it wouldn't be with terms like ugly or fat, but rather with words like "My creation," "My child," and "My bride." He is safer than any man we might run to for affirmation. He is the Rock on which we can build our lives and our sense of identity.

I don't know what Jesus wrote in the sand that day. But I like to imagine that He was writing the elements of the woman's identity that others did not see, just as He writes to us about His love for us and His appreciation for our beauty in His Word. We have value. We possess beauty. We have much to offer and we are loved. These truths can be our solace.

I am happy to report that by teaching me about my beauty, Christ guided me into more loving and healthy relationships. The man I married loves Jesus, and he understands that I am the daughter of the King of kings. He treats me with the kindness and respect that I deserve, and he treasures the many parts of who I am. He also sees my beauty. Not the kind of beauty the world entices me to offer, but the true, timeless beauty that comes from the fruits of God's Spirit. He doesn't throw rocks at my heart; instead, he works hard to protect it.

In Matthew, Jesus describes each of us not as a neighborhood, but as an entire city. The city He describes is not run-down and crime-ridden. Instead it is beautiful, well protected, and set apart.

You are the light of the world. A city on a hill cannot be hidden. Neither do people light a lamp and put it under a bowl. Instead they put it on its stand, and it gives light to everyone in the house. In the same way, let your light shine before men, that they may see your good deeds and praise your Father in heaven. (Matthew 5:14–16)

You are a beautiful city. You are well lit, well taken care of, and destined to give testimony to God's glory. Even the parts of you that have been torn down by others are redeemable by Christ. You are His architectural masterpiece. It is His plan for people to look at you and praise Him. You are not a littered sidewalk. You are not a deserted neighborhood. You are not a broken window.

Your heart is not a safe place to throw stones at.

You are described as a city on a hill. The picture that comes to our minds is that of one that can be seen for miles and miles just as Christ's work in us is to have far-reaching effects.

But another aspect of this city is that it is elevated for protection. In biblical times cities needed protection. There were warring armies seeking to plunder thriving cities, so the builders of these cities became careful engineers of their city's borders and fortifications. A city on a hill was easier to protect. Enemies could be seen long before they arrived, and it took them a while to get to the city's gates because there were mountains to climb.

We need to fortify our cities as well. There are those who would seek to damage and plunder your heart and life. Take steps to protect yourself against the stones that others might be tempted to throw in your direction. Here's how:

Know the State of Your Streets

Take an honest assessment of the shape your heart is in. Are you broken? Are there places in your heart that need repair? Is your picker-outer broken? Have your feelings about your lack of worth led you into relationships that confirm that you don't have much to offer? Have you been in a series of relationships in which you have been abused or taken advantage of?

During the period of my life when my dating patterns were destructive, I simply failed to notice the pattern. I knew that my heart was being broken over and over, but I just assumed that that was normal. I started to believe that all men acted in such a way that left me wounded. I thought that friendships were supposed to be draining, that the constant sacrificing of myself and my needs was just par for the course. I was wrong.

If these patterns have emerged in your life, I want you to recognize that relationships in which you are abused, neglected, or repeatedly taken advantage of *are not healthy*. It is the nature of relationships that there is some sacrifice and give-and-take involved, but if you are gravitating toward painful relationships consistently, there is evidence of a deeper problem.

In order to know the state of your streets, you are going to have to ask yourself some tough questions. Start with asking if the relationships that are most important to you bring you more pain than joy. Be honest about whether or not your parents or other authority figures often question whether your dating choices are appropriate. Be real about whether or not your relationships leave you feeling drained and frustrated. Be honest with yourself even if it hurts. You cannot begin to clean up your neighborhood until you recognize the state your life is truly in. If your heart has become a place that invites others to throw stones, there is work to be done. The first step in the restoration process comes with acknowledging that patterns of destruction and neglect have emerged.

Fortify Your City

If you recognize that your relationships are destructive, you need to fortify the walls of your heart. Just as the city Jesus described was elevated for protection, your boundaries and standards for relationships probably need to be raised as well. It might be that there are some relationships that Christ would call you to give up or to take a break from. It is possible that you need to stop dating altogether for a while until Christ has repaired certain areas of your heart.

I am not saying that the process of protecting your heart is easy. It is not. But it is so vitally important. Proverbs 4:23 tells us, "Above all else, guard your heart, for it is the wellspring of life." We are to fight fiercely to guard our heart because it is the very core of our being. A broken heart affects every part of us, and if our hearts are broken over and over, our lives will crack.

Guarding our heart is not necessarily the same as putting up walls. I became so wounded as a result of my dating relationships that I began to believe the lie that it wasn't safe to reveal my heart to anyone. I kept everyone at arm's length. True, this kept people from hurting me as often, but I became wounded in a different way because I withdrew from or didn't allow myself the pleasure that comes from healthy relationships.

Guarding your heart means to be cautious, to honestly evaluate the benefits of the relationships you are in, and to understand your motivation for being in those relationships. And as always, we are not without a guide. Philippians 4:7 promises that "the peace of God, which transcends all understanding, will guard your hearts and your minds in Christ Jesus." Christ is able to protect us if we let Him. He is able to speak to us about appropriate boundaries for our hearts and relationships.

When we apply the broken windows theory to our lives, it becomes clear that embracing our beauty and worth is not a small issue. When we fail to see our value, it affects us in profoundly negative ways. Likewise, when we are able to trust that God's truths about our beauty and worth are real, the restoration and freedom that are available to us are powerful indeed. You are a bright light, a city on a hill. You are the work of God's hand. You are beautiful. Your heart is worth protecting. You are a living testament to the greatness of God. It is my prayer for you that you will see the beauty that lies within you and do the work to keep others from throwing stones in your direction.

JOURNAL PROMPTS

1. Who has insulted you or said unkind things about your appearance? How has that altered your perception of yourself?

2. How do you think the adulterous woman felt? What was the difference between how much value the Pharisees saw in her and Christ's perception of her worth?

3. Are there some relationships that need new boundaries in order for your heart to be fully fortified?

4

LAYING THE FOUNDATION:
THREE TRUTHS ABOUT THE BODY

I'm willing to bet that you know a lot about the human body. I remember making skeletal systems out of milk jugs in elementary school. We learned about our skulls, our femurs, and our kneecaps.

It is amazing to think about the 206 bones that exist underneath my skin. (I admit I had to look that number up. Sorry, Mrs. Fitch, I didn't remember that from second grade!)

In middle school we learned about the smallest part of the human body, the cell. I made a model of a cell out of an old hamster wheel and some clear Jell-O. (Don't ask.) The Jell-O melted all over the place on the day of my presentation, but I still remember talking about my nucleus made out of a bouncing ball and the protons and neutrons made out of dried spaghetti. Some scientists estimate that your body is composed of as many as ten trillion cells. That blows my mind.

The truth is, your body is incredible. Without much effort from us, our bodies do amazing things every day. When was the last time you told yourself, "Hey, heart, make sure you keep pumping today" or, "Hey, lungs, make sure that you keep filling with air so I don't pass out"?

Your body is a remarkable work of God's hand. As Christian women, we tend to minimize the importance of our feminine body. We are encouraged to ignore it, to turn our attention anywhere but to our own appearance. While I wholeheartedly believe that the true source of your beauty is within you (not in cells and bones, but in the depths of your heart), I also believe that your body is important. It should be celebrated, cared for, and above all, praised as a beautiful testament to God's love for His creation.

In her book *Mom, I Feel Fat!*, Sharon Hersh points out three truths about the body.[1] They are worth examining. As we explore these truths, it is my prayer that you will begin to see your body through new perspectives. Let's jump in.

Truth #1: The Body Is Important

I remember it like it was yesterday. My head hurt. I was bleeding, and my mom was really upset. I was eight, and I had just wiped out on my bicycle. My head must have hit the pavement first, and although it didn't really hurt, it was bleeding a lot. My dad was trying to clean me up, and my mom acted like I'd just been in the most tragic accident of all time (moms can be like that). I still have a scar on my forehead to remind me of my spill.

The body is amazing. If you knew me as an eight-year-old, you would know that it's a miracle that I didn't gash my head every day. I was rowdy, curious, clumsy. But my body could take it all—the climbing, the running, even the kickball. If I fell, I got up. If I got a cut, it healed. It's not that I am particularly resilient; it's that God designed all of our bodies with wondrous precision and incredible abilities.

It is hard to imagine ourselves apart from our bodies. Our body is the vessel that houses every part of us. It seems obvious that the human body is among the most complex and marvelous works of God's creation. Your body is nothing short of awe inspiring. Whether or not you're happy with your thighs or are content with your complexion or are pleased with the specifics of the shape of your body, God crafted your physical being on purpose for a purpose.

It is your body that allows you to function. Your body provides the means for you to walk, talk, sing, dance, interact, rest, think, feel, and experience.

There is a story in the Bible that reminds us of this truth. It is the story of a woman whose body isn't functioning normally.

As a result, her world is changed. She reaches out to the Savior for help. Let's check it out.

 A large crowd followed and pressed around [Jesus]. And a woman was there who had been subject to bleeding for twelve years. She had suffered a great deal under the care of many doctors and had spent all she had, yet instead of getting better she grew worse. When she heard about Jesus, she came up behind him in the crowd and touched his cloak, because she thought, "If I just touch his clothes, I will be healed." Immediately her bleeding stopped and she felt in her body that she was freed from her suffering. (Mark 5:24–29)

Imagine what her life was like. She had been hemorrhaging for twelve years. She had spent everything to get well, but received no relief, and in fact, got worse. The Bible said that she "suffered a great deal." She may even have been isolated, since it was unlikely that many people wanted to spend time with a woman in her condition. The good news is that Jesus, the Great Physician, intervened.

What do you think she did next? If I were her I would have danced all the way home!

Maybe your body has a handicap and some tasks are a challenge. Maybe you have a recurring or chronic condition or physical weakness. Or maybe not. In any case, your body is an important, even essential, part of who you are.

God's creation never ceases to astound me. Have you ever stopped to think about why He created us the way He did? I think that many aspects of the way we are created are wonderful—unnecessarily wonderful! He could have designed the human body to just do the essentials: breath, move, eat, and so on. But He went way beyond that. God engineered our bodies in a way that allows us to experience the world around us to the fullest.

Think about it. He didn't have to give us five senses. But He did. Because of the way He designed our bodies, we are able to smell bread baking, taste fresh strawberries, see mountains and oceans, feel the touch of others, and hear beautiful music.

He didn't have to craft us so that we required rest. But I am so glad that He did. Can you imagine if your life went continuously along like one never-ending day? I don't know about you, but there are lots of problems in my life that don't look so daunting after a good night's rest. The truth is that God formed your body in a way that allows you to enjoy your life. Your body is a wonderful gift.

 That's not all. As females, our bodies are particularly important because we have been given the very God-like ability to birth life. I went to the doctor with Nikki, my twin, when she was just a few months along in her pregnancy. The doctor found the baby's heartbeat, which sounded like a wind tunnel to me. That tiny heart beating inside of my sister's womb was just amazing! A few months later Nikki showed me the sonogram. I could see my niece sucking her thumb even though she was still in utero.

After the baby was born, my sister told me that giving birth to her was a powerful, almost indescribable experience. "It was like magic," she said. "It was the most amazing thing I've ever done."

Whether or not we personally experience giving birth, the fact that our bodies were designed with such an ability confirms the importance of our physical selves.

Why is it important to convince you that your body is important? Because I want you to know that it is okay to value your body and your outward appearance. There are lots of steps you can take to take care of your body. Good hygiene, fitness, and fashion, for example, are all tools you can use to take care of what God has given you.

I don't know about you, but as a Christian woman sometimes I feel like it's not acceptable for me to focus on my body. I might feel guilty if I relax with a long bath or if I spend too much time shopping for clothes. Maybe I should be focusing on more spiritual things, I think. While it's true that there is more to our real selves than the physical, and our focus should be more on spiritual things, it is still okay to recognize that it is God who created our bodies, and our bodies therefore matter.

Truth #2: The Body Is Not All There Is

A second truth to recognize is that the body is not all there is. Recognizing that our bodies matter is one thing, but obsessing over them is another. That is where so many of us run into trouble. You are not defined simply by your body alone. God has given you gifts, abilities, and passions that are more of a reflection of your worth than what size jeans you wear or whether or not your clothes are the up-to-the-minute style.

Proverbs 31, one of the most powerful chapters in Scripture, is brought to a close with the portrait of what a noble woman looks like. These verses are rich with instruction of what a godly woman is like, but they also point out an important truth about our physical appearance.

Proverbs 31:30 points out that "Charm is deceptive, and beauty is fleeting; but a woman who fears the Lord is to be praised."

Did you catch it? What word does the author use to describe beauty? Fleeting. Temporary. Short-lived. Gone in a flash. It's true. We will all age, no matter how much beauty cream we use and how many ab crunches we subject ourselves to. So let's spend our time cultivating that which is lasting. We'll talk more about this important truth later.

Truth #3: Your Body Is a Temple

I admit it. I am a history nerd. I get lost in museums. People of the past interest me, so I am intrigued by pirates, pilgrims, and pioneers. I guess that's why I am an Old Testament junkie.

One of my favorite things to study in the Old Testament is the ark of the covenant. The writers of the Bible tell some exciting stories about it.

This ark wasn't huge, like Noah's ark; it was a physical box that symbolized the presence and power of God. Studying it reveals deep truths about our own worth.

There is a story told in 1 Samuel about the Israelites' return to camp after a brutal day of fighting the Philistines. According to Scripture, about four thousand Israelites had died in the battle, and the nation's elders were left wondering why the Lord had allowed them to be defeated. They decided to bring the ark of the covenant into their camp so that the presence of God would bring them victory.

Scripture records that when the ark arrived, the Israelites praised God so loudly that the ground shook. They knew! They knew that the ark stood for the very presence of the Lord Almighty. They knew that the presence of the ark meant the presence of their powerful God.

The Philistines knew too.

"When they learned that the ark of the Lord had come into the camp, the Philistines were afraid. 'A god has come into the camp,' they said. 'We're in trouble!'" (1 Samuel 4:6–7).

But they rallied despite their fear, and the Philistines won the battle the next day, and worse, they captured the treasured ark of the covenant from the Israelites. But God's power was revealed. God brought plagues upon the Philistines during the seven months they had the ark until they couldn't stand it anymore. They returned the ark to Israel.

That's the short version. The Bible records this story more elaborately in 1 Samuel 4–6.

This powerful box was no ordinary thing. It was created with painstaking precision. It was beautiful. In Exodus, the creation of the ark is described in great detail. Stick with me here, and God will use these details to speak truth into your heart about your own value.

Bazalel made the ark of acacia wood—two and a half cubits long, a cubit and a half wide, and a cubit and a half high. He overlaid it with pure gold, both inside and out, and made a gold molding around it. He cast four gold rings for it and fastened them to its four feet, with two rings on one side and two rings on the other. Then he made poles of acacia wood and overlaid them with gold. And he inserted the poles into the rings on the sides of the ark to carry it. He made the atonement cover of pure gold—two and a half cubits long and a cubit and a half wide. Then he made two cherubim out of hammered gold at the ends of the cover. He made one cherub on one end and the second cherub on the other; at the two ends he made them of one piece with the cover. The cherubim had their wings spread upward, overshadowing the cover with them. The cherubim faced each other, looking toward the cover. (Exodus 37:1–9)

I told you I was a history nerd. I know you're wondering, "What does that have to with me? With my body?"

Since the dawn of the new covenant (the basis of the new covenant is the death and resurrection of Christ), the same powerful God who caused the Philistines to tremble has found a new dwelling place.

Do you not know that your body is a temple of the Holy Spirit, who is in you, whom you have received from God? You are not your own; you were bought at a price. Therefore honor God with your body. (1 Corinthians 6:19–20)

If you have named Christ as your Savior, you are His temple. You are His dwelling place. He is the same powerful God who plagued the Philistines, and He has chosen to make your heart His home. You were crafted with precision equal to that given to the ark of the covenant. He knows how many cubits by how many cubits you are. He has inlaid you with beautiful things, and commands His angels to stand guard over you to protect His presence in your life. (Read Psalm 91:11.) You, sweet sister, are the temple of the Most High God. You hold His divine presence.

There's more. Remember what 1 Corinthians says: "You were bought at a price." Temples cost money. In your case, the opportunity to dwell in your heart cost Christ everything when He died on the cross. Would He have paid that price if you were worthless to Him? Would He pay the ultimate price for someone who is "too fat," "too ugly," or "too flawed" to be His temple for Him to dwell in? Somehow I doubt it.

Your body is a temple. You are God's dwelling place, and He says in Psalm 84:1, "How lovely is your dwelling place, O Lord Almighty!"

♡ JOURNAL PROMPTS

1. Who you are is more than your physical appearance. What else defines you? Begin to brainstorm about your dreams, your hopes, your talents, and everything else about your inner self.

2. Are there any habits that you need to change to take better care of your body? What are they?

3. What do you think of when you think of the word *temple*? How does it change the way you feel about yourself to understand that you are God's temple?

1. Some of my dreams are to...
   - become either a psychologist, graphic designer, or writer
   - move to canada
   - inspire people (through dance or writing)
   - become a better dancer
   - be happy with myself

Talents- i wouldn't say i have any talents, no special talents at least. everything that i may be good at could always use improvement

2. There are many.
   - eat NORMALLY!
   - eat healthy
   - work out consistently (do NOT over excercise)
   - STRETCH
   - don't overeat

3. When i think of the word "temple" i think of something very elaborate and fancy, and i certainly don't associate it with myself. It makes me feel a bit better about myself to know that i am of that much value to god. However, it also

makes me feel guilty because
I do not take proper care of
my body and sometimes hurt
it intentionally. I certainly don't
want to do that if my body
and I are of that much value
to god, but I do.
   It also makes me feel a lot
of pressure to keep doing things
right

5

WHERE DO THESE FEELINGS COME FROM?
HOW DO WE DEVELOP A SENSE OF WORTH?

Some of my earliest memories are of strangers doting on my sister Nikki and me because we were twins. In grocery stores and shopping malls strangers would peer into our stroller and comment on how we looked so much alike. Some people didn't think of us as individuals and simply referred to us as "the twins."

But I eventually learned that I was someone who was both an individual, unique in my own right, and someone who was born with a twin. That was my identity.

In first grade I liked to chase boys around the playground. Soon I was labeled "boy crazy," and that label stuck with me for years. The more people called me a flirt, the more I flirted, and the more people pointed out that I was boy crazy, the crazier about boys I became.

When I was eight, I watched my mom diet and exercise and heard her talk about the fact that she didn't like her weight. I assumed that dieting was something all women did, even a woman as beautiful as my mom.

Sometimes when I was riding in the car with my father, he would whistle in appreciation when he noticed a thin woman. He would do the same thing when he saw an attractive and slender woman on television. His behavior taught me that thin equals beautiful and that to draw attention from a man I needed to be skinny.

When I was ten, my parents divorced and I learned that I was "leaveable." I didn't understand what was happening to my family, but I had a sneaking suspicion that if I had been a better kid, things would have turned out differently. I vowed to be good in the hope that things would change, and I learned that I could never quite be good enough.

In junior high I often found myself in the middle of a catfight. On top of the discovery that girls can be mean, I learned that in order to protect myself, I needed to be mean back. I developed a quick wit and a sharp tongue. I learned that these could be powerful weapons.

By high school I learned that achievements in the classroom and in sports led to praise. I interpreted this to mean that the more I accomplished, the more I was worth.

When I was nineteen, I read an article that said Jennifer Aniston had once been a struggling actress who weighed 135 pounds —far too heavy for Hollywood standards! So she hired a trainer and lost weight and watched the offers for acting jobs, including her role as Rachel on *Friends*, come pouring in. I weighed exactly 135 pounds at the time I read that article, so I decided that my weight was hindering me from accomplishment.

Later that year, I all but stopped eating. I lost a lot of weight and people started to notice. I got a lot of attention and a lot of compliments. I was reminded that thin equaled beautiful, and I learned that no price was too high to pay to be thin. As my body shrank and the compliments increased, I also learned that there was no such thing as *too* thin.

When I was twenty-two, I regained a lot of weight. I was happily married and enjoyed cooking for my new hubby. I was also beginning my career, and I was working too hard to think about exercise and eating a healthy diet. People apparently figured that out, because I started to hear subtle comments about my clothes not fitting the same as they used to. I became terrified that everyone noticed my weight gain. When I looked in my closet I cried, because I saw clothes that didn't fit my new frame.

I became convinced that I was worth less if I weighed more.

My development of my sense of worth has been a journey. So has yours. There have been many defining moments when my family or my friends or my culture have sent me a message that I have interpreted to mean something specific about my worth. Years of comments and suggestions and articles and advertisements have sent tiny but persistent signals to my heart about who I am. In many cases, I simply misinterpreted those signals. My dad's whistles at beautiful women on television weren't intended to define *me*. An article about Jennifer Aniston wasn't written to point out that *I* was too heavy, but I misread the signal and developed a flawed sense of worth.

Your identity has been developed over time through a series of signals, just like mine has.

If you are fortunate to have a healthy sense of your worth, there is a reason for that. And if your sense of identity is flawed, there is a reason for that as well. These signals we've been receiving are like a road map on our hearts. So where do your feelings of worth or inadequacy come from? What does your road map look like?

Following the Signs

There are certain mile markers that affect our development in the area of worth. Each of us has been influenced by various sources, including our parents, our culture, and our experiences. From very early on, our interactions with these sources—or our perceptions of our interactions—shape our sense of identity. By examining the road map that has been left on our hearts in these areas, we gain an understanding of why we feel the way that we do about ourselves. Perhaps more important, if we are able to look critically at the way we have interpreted signals about our worth throughout our lifetime, we can identify areas where we misread the signs and arrived at a perception of ourselves that is flawed.

So let's get out our maps. Are you willing to think critically about the individuals and circumstances that have shaped your sense of worth? Is it possible that you've been going down the wrong road all along? That you've simply driven in the wrong direction in some areas of your sense of self because you misunderstood what was being communicated to you? Together, let's explore the major mile markers that shape my sense of worth and yours. Consider it a road trip . . . I'll even bring the snacks!

The Father Factor

Our fathers play no small role in our sense of self. In fact, for many of us, the father factor is a critical element in our development of our sense of worth. We are wired to desire affirmation from our fathers. When that affirmation is freely given, we tend to develop a healthy sense of worth and healthy boundaries in our relationships with other men.

But when our dads are distant or cold or demanding or absent, we tend to interpret that to mean that there is something wrong with us. Fatherhood wounds are very powerful tools in the shaping of our sense of worth, and we often misinterpret them to mean that we are flawed.

I adored my dad as a little girl. I wanted to marry him. I needed to have one of his T-shirts with me to snuggle in order to sleep. He was kind and attentive, and I felt safe, secure, and cherished.

But when my dad decided to leave our family, I was left deeply wounded. My ten-year-old heart couldn't understand why he didn't love me enough to stay, and I assumed that there must be something terribly wrong with me. This was a major fork in the road to my development of worth. I spent years trying to be good enough, thin enough, smart enough, and pretty enough to make sure that no one else would ever leave.

I got so wrapped up in being enough that I lost the freedom to just be myself.

What about you? Did your dad affirm that you are beautiful and loveable? If so, be grateful, for this is foundational. If your sense of worth is healthy, there is a good chance that your dad deserves some of the credit.

But maybe your heart has been broken by your dad. Maybe he has been too critical or maybe he has put too much emphasis on your performance in school or in sports. Perhaps you have wondered if he really loves you or what more you can do to get his approval. Maybe your dad has been absent altogether, leaving you feeling abandoned and unsafe.

We often misinterpret the mistakes our dads make to mean something is wrong with *us*. This simply isn't true. My dad left our family because *he* made a poor choice. It didn't mean that something was wrong with *me*. It didn't mean that I needed to spend the rest of my life striving to be all things to all people. It didn't mean that I'm not worth sticking around for. Your dad's choices probably don't have much to do with who you are either.

Imagine that you've come to a fork in the road. One road leads us to continue to believe the lies about ourselves that are rooted in negative experiences with our earthly fathers; but if we choose the other way, we can embrace the words of affirmation that our heavenly Father offers so willingly.

Our earthly fathers will never be perfect. They will mess up. They will say unkind things. They will make mistakes. But we have a heavenly Father who will not fail us. If we allow Him to be the shaper of our sense of worth, He will make our paths straight. Consider carefully what our heavenly Father reminds us of in His Word:

▶ We are God's children (Romans 8:16).

▶ He considers us valuable (Matthew 6:26).

▶ He desires to give us good gifts (Matthew 7:11), even more than our earthly dads desire to do the same.

▶ James 1:17 says that He does not change. Therefore His feelings about us do not change. He will not leave us. He won't admire us one minute and ignore us the next. He is a flashing neon sign on our road trip to discover who we are, and He announces clearly that we are loved.

The Mom Mark

Our moms aren't off the hook. They play an equally powerful role in how we perceive ourselves. For many of us, our moms are our primary teachers of the definition of beauty. If our mom is at peace with her beauty, we are more likely to feel free to embrace the beauty that we have to offer. But if we watch our mom struggle to feel beautiful, we learn to struggle as well.

My mom is stunning. She has finally found peace with her beauty, but it has been a long road. During my childhood she tried Jenny Craig, Weight Watchers, the cabbage soup diet, and just about any other plan that might help her shed a few pounds. I saw her make faces in the mirror and tug at her clothes in a way that sent a signal that she was feeling insecure. I learned to do the same.

Mommas who struggle to embrace their worth often raise daughters who struggle in the area of beauty. This truth was recently addressed by a reader of *Self* magazine.

She wrote, "Parents don't always realize how their ideas about their weight and food can affect their children. My mom has been dieting off and on in an unhealthy manner for most of my life, while my dad always managed to point out overweight women. I learned from both of them that appearance is worth more than health or happiness. Parents: Think about what you say and do. Your kids are listening and watching."[1]

She's right. We are watching, aren't we? And many of us have misinterpreted our mother's struggle with beauty to mean that our own beauty is somehow flawed. Debra Waterhouse points out that for many moms and daughters a dangerous pattern has emerged.

"More mothers are dieting; more daughters are dieting. More mothers are disordered eaters; more daughters are disordered eaters. More mothers are overweight; more daughters are overweight. This sequence is not coincidental."[2]

Likewise, a mom who embraces her own beauty and worth gives her daughter permission to see that she is beautiful. If your mom loves and accepts her beauty, she has given you a precious gift by teaching you to do the same.

Again, if we pull out our road maps and take a look at the twists and turns that have been directed by our moms, we have a choice. We can either continue patterns of dislike and frustration with our beauty that we have learned from watching our moms, or we can choose a different path. We can break free from the lies that all women diet or that dissatisfaction with our bodies is normal, and we can head in the direction of self-love and self-acceptance.

The Power of Suggestion

Many of us wear labels that have been assigned unintentionally. People take notice of our accomplishments, and we feel driven to continue to excel in order to gain praise. Or our friends and family members make observations about us, and we spend years trying to prove them right or wrong. We work hard to live up to the perceptions of others and often fail to nurture our true selves.

What labels are you wearing? Do you feel pressure to play sports because you have been labeled a star athlete? Do you question your intelligence because somewhere along the line someone suggested you weren't smart? Are you the pretty one in your family who doesn't have the freedom to concentrate on areas other than appearance? Have the words of others shaped your sense of identity and worth?

For many of us, our sense of self has been hugely influenced by the opinions of others. This is not always bad. Sometimes the people around us can see parts of us that we cannot see. They might recognize a gift and encourage us to nurture it, or praise our strengths in a way that helps develop a healthy self-concept. But sometimes there is danger found in the labels that are assigned to us. It is possible for us to believe things about ourselves that simply aren't true. It is also possible for us to spend our time behaving in a way that affirms our labels even when those labels weren't accurate to begin with.

J. K. Rowling, the author of the Harry Potter series, writes about the influence of the labels she and her sister bore as children.

"Di had—and still has—very dark, almost black hair, and dark brown eyes like my mother's, and she was considerably prettier than I was (and she still is). As compensation, I think, my parents decided that I must be 'the bright one.' We both resented our labels. I really wanted to be less freckly-beach-ball-like, and Di, who is now a lawyer, felt justifiably annoyed that nobody had noticed she was not just a pretty face. This undoubtedly contributed to the fact that we spent about three quarters of our childhood fighting like a pair of wildcats imprisoned together in a very small cage."[3]

When others suggest who we are, we have a tendency to believe them. Years of subtle (and not so subtle) comments and suggestions add up to a definition of ourselves that isn't always accurate. This path toward self-definition reminds me of the house built on the sand that Jesus talks about in Matthew 7:26–27. Jesus tells His followers, "But everyone who hears these words of mine and does not put them into practice is like a foolish man who built his house on sand. The rain came down, the streams rose, and the winds blew and beat against that house, and it fell with a great crash."

WE DON'T NEED TO PROVE THAT WE ARE BEAUTIFUL AND VALUABLE.

Building our sense of self on the labels assigned to us by others is the same as building on a shaky foundation like sand; and when something happens to shake that foundation, our houses crash down around us. By then it should be clear that we have headed in the wrong direction.

This is not to say that we have no responsibility in our perceptions of ourselves. While it is true that others have influenced how we see ourselves and our beauty, ultimately it is our responsibility to either embrace God's truth about our beauty or to continue to take our signals from others.

No matter what messages have been sent to us by others, it is sinful to make beauty an idol . . . and equally dangerous to believe that our worth is flawed, despite God's clear message to the contrary. It is Jesus who ascribes to us our worth. No matter what others may say about us, we don't need to prove that we are beautiful and valuable.

Jesus saw the map that had been drawn on my heart. He knew that I misunderstood my worth and had misinterpreted the signs sent by others. Because He is loving and compassionate, He decided to show me a different path, a path marked by His truth for my life. He laid a road marked with signs that acknowledged that I was loved and loveable, valued, and equipped with the gifts and abilities that God intended me to have.

What does He see when He looks at the road map of your heart? Do you lack direction? Is your path toward self-acceptance a straight one? Or have you been distracted by the voices of others?

I encourage you to take an honest look at your sense of your own identity. Study the signs, and determine who has influenced your path. And then allow the Lord to speak His truth over you about your worth in His eyes. If you allow who you are *in Christ* to be the core of your identity, I promise it will make the trip much sweeter.

1. What are the major stops on the road map of your identity?

2. Have you misinterpreted some of the signals sent by others in the area of your worth? Ask Christ to replace those areas of confusion with His truth.

3. What labels do you bear? How did you get those labels? What labels would you like to bear?

6

MIXED MESSAGES:
SIFTING THROUGH THE GLOSSY PRINT

I had just got out of the bathtub. One of my favorite ways to relax after a long day is to take a leisurely soak in my Jacuzzi (that bathtub is the reason we bought our house!). I love to fill the water with fragrant bubbles, light some candles, grab a magazine, and spend time catching up on the latest fashions without the distractions of work and family.

But this time, when the water turned cold and I got out, I stared critically at my body in the mirror. I took a very long time getting dressed because nothing looked quite right. I made a mental note that I needed to go shopping soon. I spent forever trying to get my hair to look picture-perfect. I never did quite achieve the movie-star glamour I was hoping for. I felt frustrated, flawed, and frumpy.

I wondered, "Why am I feeling this way? Where did this sudden bout with insecurity come from?"

I looked on the floor and saw the magazine I'd been reading. The water from the tub had curled the pages, but I could still read the headlines about beauty, fashion, and relationships. Could it be that the fun fashion magazines I'd just admired during my soak did more than entertain me? Surely such magazines are just harmless fun, right?

A flip through TV channels produces the same results. I notice that I don't really look like the girls I see on the screen. They are slimmer and more beautiful than I am. Their hair is perfect. Their skin looks flawless. Their clothes don't look anything like the outfits I wear. I really need to hit the mall!

Driving down the highway, I meet the same flawless faces—only this time they are huge. On billboards placed all along the road, giant images of perfection remind me that I am ordinary. They make me want to buy skin creams and tanning packages in order to be transformed into a more magnificent beauty.

These reactions to the media aren't rare for me. I often feel frustrated with myself when I am exposed to the media's portrayal of a beautiful woman. Advertisers are banking on the fact that I am not the only one feeling this way. In fact, researchers have found that 70 percent of the women who look at fashion magazines reported feeling depressed, guilty, and ashamed of their bodies after less than five minutes of flipping through the pages of those magazines.[1] Additional research has linked exposure to the unrealistically thin, young, and often airbrushed female bodies consistently portrayed in the media to depression, loss of self-esteem, and the development of eating disorders in women of all ages. The multibillion-dollar diet, fashion, and advertising industries are counting on my insecurities to sell everything from razors to sports cars. In fact, they are cashing in big-time on the insecurities of entire generations.

They are lying to me about my worth. They are lying to you about your beauty, and we are falling for it hook, line, and sinker.

Our number one Enemy in the fight to embrace our worth is Satan, and it's true that the root of this issue is spiritual. We'll talk about that more extensively later in the book. But the world around us plays no small role in shaping our beauty ideals and our perceptions of ourselves.

It is no secret that the women we see in magazine covers and in television commercials don't look like the average woman. But what you may not realize is how intentional and deceptive the media's portrayal of beauty really is.

In order to cut through the lies that the media is telling us about our beauty, we need to get real about the ways that the media affects us. We are exposed to over two thousand ads a day,[2] and most of us will spend one and a half years of our lives watching television commercials. It is naive of us to think that this exposure won't affect us, and when we look at the ways our beauty and worth are portrayed in most advertisements, it is easy to see that the effect is largely negative.

Marketers are intentional about making you feel insecure in the area of your beauty. They are investing billions of dollars developing new ways to shape your heart and mind. For many of us, media has become our biggest influence. The results are disastrous. Let's take a magnifying glass to the world of advertising and search out the lies that advertisers are feeding us. I bet that there is a lot that you didn't realize about the television and magazine ads that have become such a prominent part of your world.

You Are the Target

Teenagers and young adults are in the crosshairs of many advertisers' marketing weapons. They are specifically targeting you. Their advertisements are carefully crafted to draw you in. Why? Because research has shown them that you are vulnerable and that you have money to spend.

One marketing observer pointed out that advertisers intentionally prey on young people because you are naturally insecure during this season of life. "Marketing is especially powerful in the lives of our teens. The teenage years are characterized by change. Because the change brings confusion, kids spend time wondering where the changes taking place in their lives are going to end," he said. "And they wonder if the ending for them will yield something that leads to their acceptance by others. Consequently, the teenage years are marked by an insecurity that leads to them being easily influenced if influence promises to help them fulfill their hopes, dreams, and emptiness. In other words, teenagers are perfect targets for the marketing machine."[3]

In a similar statement, a marketing executive admitted that advertisers are working overtime to convince you that you need their product to have worth.

"Advertising at its best is making people feel that without their product, you're a loser," she said. "Kids are very sensitive to that. If you tell them to buy something, they are resistant. But if you tell them that they'll be a dork if they don't, you've got their attention. You open up emotional vulnerabilities, and it's very easy to do with kids because they are the most emotionally vulnerable."[4]

The reality is that advertisers are literally sitting around the boardroom table developing strategies to profit from your weaknesses. They have studied you and your peers. They know the challenges that you face, and they are bent on turning those challenges into marketing dollars.

Does this make you feel exposed? Does it frustrate you that marketers are intentionally trying to convince you that you are a loser? Are you angry about the fact that companies are willing to pounce on your insecurities in order to dip into your wallet? Me too. But there's more.

They Are Targeting Your Beauty

Advertisers aren't just targeting you in general. They are specifically working to convince you that your beauty is flawed. They are intentionally sending you the message that you aren't beautiful. Their goal is to convince you that you need their product in order to be beautiful. They aren't making you feel insecure by accident. It is premeditated and planned.

Marketing has added fuel to the fire of our body-conscious culture, and it has driven you to look in the mirror with critical eyes. The hope of advertisers is that when you look in the mirror you will be dissatisfied with your own reflection because you are comparing yourself to a beauty standard that you've seen over and over again in magazines, television, and movies.

Marketers intentionally use women who are thinner than average and more attractive than most to make us feel unlovely. They are counting on us to react to those feelings by spending money. Often we do. But the feelings of emptiness remain. There is real danger in comparing ourselves to the images of perfection that advertisers offer.

If we were to look to Christ and ask the question "Who's the fairest of them all?" He would gush about His love for us and His careful crafting of our beauty. If we use the media as our mirror, the answer is sure to be "someone else." And that someone is likely to be a carefully engineered image of perfection that we will never obtain.

It's a Fake

The images on television and in magazines are not only purposefully created to pique your attention, but in most cases they are fake. Every single aspect of an advertisement is engineered to send you a specific message. The lighting is planned. The placement of people and objects is planned. The colors are strategic. Most models are airbrushed and Photoshopped so that no imperfections can be seen. Blemishes are removed, tummies are flattened, thighs are trimmed, and the final product—a seemingly perfect woman—is what we see in the magazine or on television. But what we're seeing isn't reality. Reality is more likely an ordinary woman made up to look extraordinary.

Celebrities know that the way they are being portrayed isn't real. Some have started to speak out against it. Jamie Lee Curtis spoke out publicly several years ago about the false image the world offers. She created quite a buzz by offering to pose without lighting or makeup for an issue of *More* magazine. She refused to be airbrushed or Photoshopped. By offering her true beauty, Ms. Curtis helped to expose the craftiness of marketers, and she proved that the beauty that the magazines are selling us is unattainable.

Actress Kate Winslet openly shared her similar frustration after *GQ* altered a picture of her for their cover. She admitted that the tiny thighs that were shown didn't belong to her. The images of her body were altered after the photo shoot to make her appear thinner that she really is.

"The retouching is excessive," Kate says. "I do not look like that and more importantly I don't desire to look like that."[5]

But these women are rare. Most of the cover girls we see never admit that their images have been changed, leaving us to believe that there is something wrong with us because we don't look like they do. It is a bold and terrible lie. The beauty that the world offers isn't real, and it is a cheap substitute for the beauty that we already possess because Christ created it in us. No amount of airbrushing or computer alteration can compare to the beauty crafted by the Creator.

Letting Christ Shape Our Worldview

We aren't the first ones to allow the messages of the world to seep into our hearts. Through His Word, God has warned believers to avoid the pollution that the world offers (see James 1:27).

First John 2:15 tells us not to love the world or anything in the world. Verse 16 goes on to remind us that "everything in the world—the cravings of sinful man, the lust of his eyes and the boasting of what he has and does—comes not from the Father but from the world."

Our cravings to possess worldly beauty, our lust to look like the women we see in the media, and the images of perfection that the world boasts about don't come from our Father. The beauty that the world offers cannot satisfy, and we should be intentional about guarding our hearts against it.

Romans 12:2 offers similar guidance. "Do not conform any longer to the pattern of this world, but be transformed by the renewing of your mind." James 4:4 cuts to the chase by reminding us that "friendship with the world is hatred toward God."

Many of us maintain a casual friendship with the world

through our media usage. We spend more time digesting the messages that the media offers than we do seeking the truth of Christ. We allow the media to shape our hearts and lives. Instead of allowing Christ to shape our worldview, we fall for the media messages offered by the world. We maintain a love affair with worldly beauty instead of embracing God's truth about our worth. We seek out media and marketing as a means to fill the God-shaped holes in our hearts. The results are hollow.

HERE ARE SOME PASSAGES YOU CAN REFLECT ON WHEN YOU NEED A REMINDER THAT YOU ARE KNOWN BY YOUR CREATOR AND LOVED BY HIM.

- Psalm 139
- 1 Peter 5:7
- Philippians 4:4-8
- Luke 12:6-7
- Matthew 18:12-14

"We are empty until the hole in our soul is filled by a relationship with God through his Son Jesus Christ and we are living under the rule and reign of God," writes Walt Muller in an article about what parents and teens need to know about marketing. "Marketing plays into this and exploits that emptiness and yearning by promising redemption, ful- fillment, wholeness and satisfaction through the purchase and use of products. In effect, marketing substi- tutes a false gospel for the true gospel. If we believe marketing's promise to deliver—promises that in fact never can deliver—we run the risk of falling into the endless cycle of believing the lies and buying product after product in the hope that somehow, this time, we will be fulfilled." [6]

God doesn't warn us to break off our friendship with the world because He seeks to rob us of good things. He doesn't speak out against conformity to the world's standards to make us strange and cut off from our culture. He is seeking to protect us from the false gods who cannot save us. Fulfillment cannot come from anything we can buy, and true beauty cannot come from any other source but Christ.

I am not suggesting that we cut all ties with the media. That would be nearly impossible. But I am asking you to guard your heart against marketing messages that are deceptive and harmful. There are certain magazines that we should be avoiding because of the reactions they cause us to have. We should turn the TV off when certain television shows where women are portrayed unrealistically are aired. We should be careful not to fill the voids in our hearts with stuff. And above all, we need to learn to view the media through the lens of Christ's truth that we are loved and lovely. We need to acknowledge that the world is seeking to deceive us, and work to put some boundaries into our friendship with the world's beauty messages.

Tonight I am going to take another long soak in the tub. I'll light candles and pour in some yummy-smelling soap. But I think I'll leave the magazines on the shelf. There is rest to be found in fasting from the images of the world. Instead of allowing myself to be targeted by marketers who seek to convince me that I am not enough, I think I will take a soak in the messages of my beauty offered so graciously by Christ.

10 Tips for Devotional Reading

Be sure you're spending more time with God's Word than you are with magazines, television, and other sources of messages that may not be true and healthy. Here are some ways to get the most out of your personal Bible study and prayer time.

Read a Proverb a day

There are 31 chapters in the book of Proverbs and 31 days in most months. Starting on the first day of the month, read a chapter from Proverbs each day. Each one is packed full of insights for living a life that is pleasing to the Lord.

Journal

Write out your prayers in the form of letters to God. Then, search the Word for verses that provide wisdom, encouragement, or answers to the situations you wrote about. Write those verses near your journal entries. You will be amazed as you read back at past journal entries how faithful the Lord is and how powerful the Word is when applied to your life.

Pick a spot

Find a quiet, comfortable place in your house where you can concentrate on being with the Lord. Maybe it's a big comfy chair in your living room, or a quiet spot on your back deck. If your house is particularly hectic, the bathtub might prove to be your best escape. Set this space apart as sacred and use it regularly as a place to come into God's presence.

Pick a time

Find the time when you are least rushed and most able to focus, and commit to spending that time with God each day. If you find it hard to think clearly in the morning, that probably isn't the best time for you to get serious about prayer and Bible study. Instead of watching T.V. or surfing the net during the late night hours when you are most awake, set that time aside for reading your Bible. If you wake up feeling awake and alert, spend the first few minutes of your day in the Word. Try to spend time with God approximately the same time each day and make a commitment that you won't go to bed until you've read your Bible.

Pick a partner

Ask a Christian friend to be your accountability partner in this area. Encourage her to ask you weekly if you have been faithfully spending time in prayer and Bible study. Do the same for her. Get together regularly at your favorite coffeehouse or restaurant to share about what you're learning in the Word and what God is teaching you during your prayer time.

Celebrate God's creation

Pack up your Bible and journal and head outside. Find a lake, a flower-filled meadow, or a hiking trail and dig into passages about God's role as the Creator. You will likely experience His presence and His Word in new and exciting ways when you surround yourself with the sights and sounds of His creation.

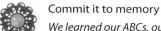

Commit it to memory

We learned our ABCs, our friends' phone numbers, and the quadratic formula the same way: We repeated them over and over in our minds, through our speech and often in writing. Nothing is more important to learn than the Word of God. Work to memorize Scripture. You may find that when you repeat verses over and over, they take on new meaning as they begin to saturate your heart and mind.

Focus on the red letters

If you aren't sure what to read during your quiet time, focus on the words of Jesus. Often His exact words will be highlighted in red in your Bible. Jesus is the way, the truth and the life (John 14:6). His words are the source of truth and guidance. When you aren't sure what to read, focus on what He has to say to you.

Dig deeper

Do a study on words or subjects in Scripture: What does the Bible say about the tongue (speech)? Baptism? Rules? Clothing? Heaven? God's sovereignty? Holiness? Friendship? Prayer? Look for answers to these topics in the Word. I promise, the research will challenge you, and as you dig deeper, I bet that your appetite for Truth will increase.

Find great resources

There are tons of Bible studies available to help guide and enhance your personal studies. Head off to your nearest Christian bookstore and spend some time digging through them. Look for studies that focus on topics you're interested in, present information in a conversational style, and require you to spend sizeable amounts of time in the Word. Here are a few recommendations to get you started:

- Experiencing God *by Henry Blackaby and Claude V. King*

- A Call to Die *by David Nasser*

- Lies Young Women Believe *by Nancy Leigh DeMoss and Dannah Gresh and the* Lies Young Women Believe *companion guide by Erin Davis*

♡ JOURNAL PROMPTS

1. Which advertisements have you seen that cause you to question your beauty? Be specific. How do they make you feel insecure?

2. How does it make you feel to know that advertisers are intentionally targeting you and your beauty? What can you do to fight back?

3. What boundaries can you establish to guard your heart against the distorted beauty messages the world offers?

7

IMPERFECT?
JOIN THE CROWD: BORN TO BE FLAWED

What are your flaws? I don't mean that you get cranky when you're tired or that you can't understand algebra no matter how hard you try (me neither). I mean physically, what drives you crazy about yourself? Is it something minor—like your hair is curly and you'd rather it was straight? Is it something major, like an abnormality that makes people stare at you, or a birthmark that everyone notices and feels the need to point out? Is it your weight? Your skin? Your height?

I have more than a few physical flaws and they drive me nuts. My weight is a biggie—you should have already picked up on that. I hate my belly. I always look about three months pregnant, and I am afraid people are constantly wondering if I am. I have little flaps of skin over the corners of my eyes. I have never met anyone else who has them except my brother. I've spent a lot of time wishing I had the money and the courage to let a plastic surgeon remove them.

My nose looks exactly the way it did when I was two, leading everyone to tell me how cute it is. At some point, a girl likes to move past the cute phase. I am afraid my nose will always keep me from being pretty or beautiful and keep me stuck at cute forever. Physically, I am far from perfect. I bet you feel the same.

All of us have flaws. Our society tells us to get rid of them at all costs. Business is booming for plastic surgeons. You can have anything enhanced, changed, or removed. Moles, birthmarks, and blemishes can all be laser-beamed away in an afternoon.

Television shows like *Extreme Makeover* tell us that the physical attributes you're born with are easy to change and that physical perfection leads to happier lives and smiling friends and relatives.

But can we really find peace by removing our flaws? Did God make mistakes when He created those "imperfections," or did He create them intentionally for our good and His glory? Once again He calls us to measure the messages of the world against His standards. The result is the realization that our imperfections, physical and otherwise, are intentional. In fact, our God is a God who is made strong in our weakness and who has always used the flawed to do His most amazing work.

Perfection Isn't an Option

The interesting thing about flaws is that we all have them. No one is perfect. Even supermodels admit that they have been airbrushed and Photoshopped even after diet and exercise routines that lead them to be smaller than their natural body shape. I love it when they confess they have cellulite or stretch marks. It feels like a victory for all womankind. There isn't a woman on the planet who is flawless. The bottom line is that perfection frankly isn't an option for *anyone*, and that physical flaws are part of the plan that was engineered for all of us.

The question I often ask is, why? Why was I made this way? Why were you made that way? To be honest, the truth that God loves me just the way I am never did much to satisfy me. I want to know why I wasn't made like the girls who are naturally skinny with flat tummies. I want to know why He thought it was a great idea to put flaps on the corners of my eyes, and I am desperate to find out why He didn't see fit to give me a grown-up nose.

Have you asked those questions about your flaws? Do you ever want to demand, "Why did You make me this way?" or "Why can't I look like that?"

BEING TALL

IF YOU SAW ME IN PERSON YOU WOULD SEE THAT MY HEIGHT IS ONE OF MY DOMINANT PHYSICAL FEATURES. I MEASURE IN AT SIX FEET TALL. BY THE TIME I WAS TWELVE YEARS OLD I WAS ALREADY 5'9". NEEDLESS TO SAY, I WAS HEAD AND SHOULDERS ABOVE EVERYONE, INCLUDING THE BOYS. IT WAS THE TOPIC OF MORE CONVERSATIONS THAN I WOULD HAVE LIKED. ADULTS WOULD TALK TO MY MOM AND ME ABOUT WHERE MY HEIGHT CAME FROM SINCE SHE IS ONLY 5'5". THEY WERE IN COMPLETE AWE THAT SOMEONE MY AGE COULD ALREADY BE TOWERING OVER MANY OF THEM. BOYS WOULD WALK BEHIND ME IN THE SCHOOL HALLS AND I WOULD HEAR THEM WHISPER, "SHE IS SO BIG." NONE OF THIS DID MUCH FOR MY FRAGILE SELF-CONFIDENCE AS AN EMOTIONAL AND AWKWARD PRETEEN.

I WOULD ALSO COMPARE MYSELF WITH MY FRIENDS. I CAN REMEMBER TRYING ON CLOTHES OR JUST LOOKING IN THE MIRROR AS WE FIXED ONE ANOTHER'S HAIR AT SLUMBER PARTIES AND THINKING THAT I WAS HUGE. I WAS NOT JUST TALLER THAN THEY WERE, MY SHOULDERS WERE BROADER (WHICH MEANT I WAS WIDER), MY FEET WERE BIGGER, MY HANDS WERE BIGGER, AND MY FACE WAS BIGGER. ANYWAY, YOU GET THE PICTURE. I FELT LIKE NOTHING ABOUT ME WAS "CUTE" BECAUSE "CUTE" THINGS WERE LITTLE AND THAT WAS THE ONE THING I WAS NOT.

So what exactly was the point in my being this tall? I believe that God made me but I did not understand why He chose to make me so very tall. Maybe when God was weaving me together in my mother's womb He got distracted when it was time to mix together the growing gene and said, "Oops, I guess she will learn to deal with it. . . . " Well, that is not true. The truth is that God has always had a purpose for my physical structure. We are all uniquely created with a purpose. God does not do random. We know from His Word that He is a God of purpose and order. What a great thing to put your confidence in!

Come to find out, God had picked out this great man to be my spouse who is 6'6" and finds great delight in my tallness. He thinks my height is a defining factor of my beauty. In part, I was created this way for him. When I was twelve and detesting my height, I could have never imagined my 6'6" dream guy who would be looking for such a trait.

Now we are raising two beautiful girls. They too are on track to be above average when it comes to height. When they are twelve and feeling awkward about being 5'9", I will be able to confidently tell them about the great plans that will unfold for them someday that are dependent upon their most unique qualities!

Andrea Hogue, Ohio

Flaws Equal Beauty

What if we made a decision to see ourselves in a different light? What if we could stop obsessing over our flaws and start enjoying them? Is it possible that the things we like least about ourselves are really our most beautiful attributes? If we look closely, we will realize that our imperfections are really beauty marks placed strategically by the hand of God.

Kendall Payne wrote about this issue in *Mirror, Mirror*. Kendall is a Christian recording artist who is no stranger to the pressure to look like everyone else. But she points out that we were all born to be an original. She tells us, "There is a verse in the Bible that says, 'Before I formed you in the womb I knew you' (Jeremiah 1:5). God is very clear that He made us and that He knew us even then. He made us with a specific plan in mind.

"Sometimes it is hard to think that when we feel different. Sometimes we just wish we could look like everyone else, but think about how boring that would be if everyone looked the same. A bunch of copies when we're all supposed to be a bunch of originals. We honor God most when we learn to appreciate and grow in love for the unique individual He made us to be."[1]

She gives us an important reminder. God created *you*. He created *me*. He painstakingly crafted us from the beginning. Maybe we heard about God as the Creator a million times in Sunday school. Now let's go deeper: I am asking you to acknowledge that God is the Creator of your flaws and that they are no accident.

Psalm 139 describes your creation. Every detail was intentional and crafted by God's own fingers.

"For you created my inmost being; you knit me together in my mother's womb. I praise you because I am fearfully and wonderfully made; your works are wonderful, I know that full well" (Psalm 139:13–14).

Your innermost parts were knit by God. He wove the flaps over the corners of my eyes. He sewed my round tummy together. I imagine He took great delight in sculpting my nose. They weren't accidents! Scripture even calls them fearful and wonderful.

He made your flaws as well, and I doubt that He sees them as imperfections. You were also made fearfully and wonderfully and with precision by a loving God. You are His work and you are wonderful. Do you know that? Do you know it full well?

But why? Why does He give us unique traits that make us stand out from the crowd? I believe they are His fingerprint, left to remind us of His deep and abiding love for us.

In Song of Songs, the author writes, "Sixty queens there may be, and eighty concubines, and virgins beyond number; but *my* dove, my *perfect* one, is unique" (6:8–9).

The Song of Songs is believed by many Bible scholars to be a picture of God's love for His people. Written in romantic language, it tells the tale of a groom's love for his bride, but the words describe how God feels about you, and in this passage He demonstrates His delight over every characteristic that makes you stand out. Can you imagine the beauty contained in a room of sixty queens? But as the word points out, perfection can only be found in uniqueness.

"My dove, my perfect one, is unique."

All of the things that set me apart are reminders that I serve a God who was active in my creation and who cares about the smallest details. They are also the parts that make me the most beautiful because they are the traits that make me unique.

I shared with you that I have a twin sister. We look a lot alike, but she doesn't have flaps over the corners of her eyes. Her hair is naturally curly and mine is straight. She has a birthmark in the shape of Africa on her calf. I have one in the shape of Jamaica on my left hip. She's left-handed and I'm right-handed. It is the traits that make us different that make us distinct individuals, and they are constant reminders that our Creator loved us enough to build in physical differences to affirm His unique love for each of us.

Graffiti

We have learned to think of beauty using the Henry Ford mass production model. We wish that we had been rolled out on an assembly line, made to look like the models of perfection we see on television and in magazines. But God doesn't churn out beauty using identical and interchangeable components. The parts of your body that you consider flaws were created *on* purpose *for* a purpose. They are there to remind you that despite the fact that you are only one of the over six billion people on the planet, God cares for you. He crafted every part of you, down to the smallest detail.

Going Even Deeper

This truth goes far beyond our outward appearance. God thrives in our weakness. He rarely approaches the perfect with plans for greatness. Paul writes about this mysterious truth. After describing a flaw that he called a "thorn in my flesh" (2 Corinthians 12:7), he records the Lord's ability to be glorified by our imperfections.

"But he [God] said to me, 'My grace is sufficient for you, for my power is made *perfect* in weakness" (2 Corinthians 12:9).

Just as in Song of Songs, Scripture gives us the secret to perfection. But it isn't by the removal of flaws—rather, it is by allowing God's power to be demonstrated through our weaknesses.

This idea is really obvious if we take a look at the characters that God decided to use throughout the Bible. From Genesis to Revelation, God's A-Team is a bunch of average joes (and josephines!). They are physically flawed. They are emotionally flawed, and in many cases they are spiritually flawed. But God uses them to change the hearts of pharaohs, rescue His warriors, establish His kingdom, and redeem the world. Why? Because His power is made perfect in our weakness.

Hebrews 11 is often referred to as the "hall of faith." This chapter reminds us of people like Noah who built an ark because he believed the Lord when He said that rain was coming. Abraham is also in the hall because he made his home in the Promised Land and because he believed God's assurance to provide an heir even in his old age. Moses led Israel across the Red Sea. Rahab welcomed spies. Gideon and David are there, along with many others whom God called and equipped to do great things.

Maybe you learned about these heroes in Sunday school or played out their stories on felt boards or sang songs with motions about them in vacation Bible school; but when we tell and retell stories about these great characters, we tend to leave out their tremendous flaws. For example . . .

After he'd been on dry land awhile, Noah got drunk and passed out in his tent (Genesis 9:20–21). Abraham had moments of doubt, and he distorted the truth when the going got tough (Genesis 12:11–20; 17:17). Moses had serious anger management issues and they followed him throughout his life (Exodus 2:12; 6:30; Numbers 20:11–13). Before God called him to free the Israelites from their Egyptian captors, Moses committed murder. He was not a glib public speaker. When God spoke to him from a burning bush, "Moses said to the Lord, 'O Lord, I have never been eloquent, neither in the past nor since you have spoken to your servant. I am slow of speech and tongue'" (Exodus 4:10).

God didn't remove this hurdle from Moses. Instead, He opted to use Moses' life, flaws and all.

Rahab made the list, though she was a prostitute. God's choice to lead the nation to victory over the Midianites was Gideon, not only the weakest member of his family, but he came from the weakest tribe in Israel (Judges 6:15). Why didn't God go to Israel's strongest tribe and choose its strongest member? Because His power was perfected in Gideon's weakness (Judges 7).

David is considered a man after God's own heart (Acts 13:22), but his list of flaws is long. He was an adulterer and a murderer, but over and over God used him in mighty ways.

Hebrews 11:38 records "the world was not worthy of them," not because they were perfect, but because they were imperfect and God chose to use them anyway.

Jesus is the ultimate example of this truth. Though sinless, Christ was fully human. His body was as human as yours is. He needed food. He needed rest. He was prone to injury and illness just like the rest of us. He was bound to the rules of the physical world, but God used Him to redeem each of us from the pit.

It is His humanness that allows us to approach. We identify with Him because He is not a God who has never walked where we've walked, but rather a God who put on weaknesses to draw us to Him.

Hebrews records, "For we do not have a high priest who is unable to sympathize with our weakness, but we have one who has been tempted in every way, just as we are—yet was without sin. . . . He is able to deal gently with those who are ignorant and are going astray, since he himself is subject to weakness" (4:15, 5:2).

Your flaws, sweet friend, are like neon arrows pointing toward Christ. He created those flaws to make you stand out from the rest of the world and to remind us that we are weak but He is so strong.

I know that you're not perfect. Neither am I. But the Lord teaches us to delight in those things that the world labels imperfections. We don't have value in spite of our flaws. Instead, we have worth because of them.

♡ JOURNAL PROMPTS

1. What would you say are your flaws?

2. Which characters in the Bible really inspire you? What are their flaws? How does God use them for His glory?

3. How can God use your flaws for His glory?

8

BUT WHY CAN'T I LOOK LIKE SHE DOES?
STRATEGIES FOR WINNING THE COMPARISON GAME

There is a game I play whenever I am in public. I have been playing it for years. It's called fatter or skinnier, and the rules are fairly simple. I just observe the other women around me and make a mental judgment about whether I am fatter or skinnier than they are. If I am at the movies, I take a quick scan of the theatre to see where my weight ranks with other moviegoers. At the grocery store, I compare myself with the other women in the frozen foods section. I am constantly asking the question, "Am I fatter or skinnier than she is?"

My husband used to play along. The results were fascinating. I almost always made the judgment that the women around me were skinnier than I was. My husband almost always came to the opposite conclusion. He usually asserted that the women around us were heavier than I was. Now my husband is no fool. He knows better than to point out women more attractive than his wife to his wife, but most of the time his opinion reflected what he honestly thought. The truth is, we were seeing the same women but perceiving those women very differently. His view was objective. Mine was clouded by my need to compare. I was ignoring the flaws of the women around me and comparing them to every flaw I saw in myself.

I bet you've played a version of the comparison game. Maybe you are constantly judging whether or not other girls are smarter than you, or more popular or more athletic. Maybe you find yourself in constant competition with an older sibling or the flawless celebrities that grace magazine covers. Maybe you're always on the lookout to see who is taller or shorter, better or worse dressed, or more or less talented than you.

The irresistible need to compare seems to be a part of our fabric as women. In fact, most girls are masters at the art of comparison. The world around us urges us on to this game. Magazines are a paper format for comparison. For around four dollars an issue, you can see who is better or worse dressed than whom, who is fatter or skinnier than the noteworthy stars around them, or how celebrity marriages stack up to the competition. You can take quizzes to see how smart, funny, or romantic you are. But the question is, compared to whom? And while it's true that we all compare, most of us have noticed that it leaves us feeling unsatisfied . . . or worse. Often, our comparisons leave us deeply wounded.

In a magazine I was reading recently, a reader wrote in to psychologist Dr. Phil about the harmful effects of playing the comparison game.

"I can't stop feeling like a failure compared with my sisters," she wrote. She continued, "Though I know I shouldn't compare myself with others, I've spent my life emulating my sisters, and I've always wanted them to be proud of me . . . I don't want to keep feeling jealous and inadequate."[1]

This woman fell into a trap I've found myself in many times before. She used the people around her as her measuring stick and determined that she didn't measure up. As a result she ended up feeling jealous and inadequate, and I would guess that her relationship with her sisters was strained. Many of us are like this reader; we have become enslaved by our impulse to compare.

This trap has been carefully set by our Enemy, Satan. He knows that comparing ourselves with others leads to feelings of discouragement, inadequacy, and jealousy. He knows that if he can turn our focus toward those around us, he can easily distract us from the standards of God. One of the most powerful weapons in his arsenal is the sense that we are alone in these

WE HAVE BECOME ENSLAVED BY OUR IMPULSE TO COMPARE.

feelings, that we are the only one reacting this way, that no one else feels like they just can't seem to measure up.

Let's face that lie right here together. Our need to compare wasn't born in the twenty-first century. It isn't simply a result of media that pushes a version of beauty that is impossible to obtain. It's the Enemy who has been setting this trap since the beginning. A return back to God's Word shows us that many have been ensnared, often with terrible results. But once again we see that the keys to these chains come from God's truth.

If we head back to the garden, we find Satan up to the same old tricks. The snake slithered in and convinced Eve to start comparing herself to others, specifically to God. This was dangerous indeed.

"You will not surely die," the serpent said to the woman. "For God knows that when you eat of [the fruit] your eyes will be opened, and *you will be like God*, knowing good and evil" (Genesis 3:4).

"You will be like God." "What you are isn't good enough." "You need to be more like someone else." These are the foundations of this lie. Eve had all she needed and could desire, but as she looked around and noticed that God possessed knowledge she did not, she let her heart play the comparison game, and a nibble of sin followed shortly after.

The comparison game is played throughout the Bible and the consequences are painful. Cain compared the Lord's favor on his offering with the favor given to the offering of his brother, Abel. He didn't like how the scales were tipped, and he became so enraged that he murdered his brother (Genesis 4:4–8). Sarai and Hagar became so jealous of each other that a deep bitterness took root in each of their hearts. The result was division among their family (Genesis 16:1–12). King Saul became consumed with jealousy after comparing himself to David (1 Samuel 18:8–9). Even Jesus' disciples could be found comparing themselves with one another (Mark 9:33–34; Luke 9:46).

Why is comparison destructive? Why would Satan tempt us to compare ourselves to others? The answer is clear when we study the results. In every single story of comparison in the Bible, comparison led to a focus on the wrong standard. Eve let a serpent define what was good for her instead of trusting God's standard for what was best. The results were immediate and painful. She lost her home in the garden. She lost her intimacy with God. She scarred her legacy.

Her son made a similar choice. Cain forgot to be grateful for the favor he did receive from God and focused on what he thought he was missing. He lost control. He sinned. He destroyed his brother.

Sarai put her hope in what she could create. Instead of resting on the promise of God, she tried to grab good things for herself. God's standard for her life was better; His promises were enough, but comparisons muddied the waters.

God's blessings on King Saul's life were many. Instead of being grateful, he was jealous. In the end it led to destruction.

Jesus had enough love and purpose and ministry for all twelve disciples, but they wanted to establish a pecking order. They set out to outdo each other and forgot to focus on pleasing their Lord.

Comparisons result in broken hearts and fractured relationships. Often, these are the same results that arise in our lives when we give in to the need to compare. Second Corinthians 2:11 encourages us to study the schemes of the Enemy to avoid being outwitted. Let's study our Enemy's tactics in the area of comparison, so we can armor up with God's best for our lives.

When we compare ourselves to siblings, to friends, to celebrities, the results are the same. God is our standard. He is our Creator, and His affirmation of our value is worth more than riches untold. When we seek the applause of people instead of His, we are focusing on the wrong standard and settling for a cheap substitute.

This misplaced focus leads to another consequence of comparison that is equally harmful. Not only does comparison lead to a focus on the wrong standard, it also tends to water a root of pride in our hearts. When we start to compare, pride starts to grow. We become more me-focused, which leads us to become less God-focused and others-focused. Scripture has much to say about pride. We know that "God opposes the proud" (James 4:6). He will actually work against us if we have allowed pride to take root! In Proverbs 16, Scripture warns that "pride goes before destruction" (v. 18). Of course our Enemy loves it when we develop a me-focused sense of pride because the results are disastrous for us!

When we play the comparison game, we are actually violating God's commandments. As part of the Ten Commandments, God admonishes us not to covet.

You shall not covet your neighbor's house. You shall not covet your neighbor's wife, or his manservant or maidservant, his ox or donkey, or anything that belongs to your neighbor (Exodus 20:17).

To covet means to wish for earnestly or to desire something that belongs to another. I would bet that you don't necessarily struggle with the things God mentioned in the Ten Commandments (I can't think of a time when I wished for an ox or desired my neighbor's maidservant or manservant, can you?). But we're not off the hook. What if that passage read, "Don't wish for the popularity of other girls in your school" or "Don't desire the talents that have been given to others instead of you"? What if Moses had the foresight to write, "Don't spend your time looking at magazines wishing you could look like the girls you see on their pages"? I'd be caught red-handed. Simply put, comparing ourselves to others causes us to sin by leading to a longing that violates God's commandments.

It is clear that comparison is not a harmless game. But for many of us, it seems impossible to stop. Take heart, sweet girl.

Let's work together to develop some strategies for tackling our need to compare.

Step 1: Get Real

The good news is, you've already taken a huge step toward kicking this nasty habit. By simply acknowledging the harmful effects of comparison and the spiritual dimensions of jealous and critical thinking, you've taken a huge step toward taming your need to compare.

Step 2: Get a New Yardstick

Dr. Phil's advice to the reader who couldn't stop comparing herself to her sisters was simple: "Don't use their yardstick to measure your worth."[2] He's right. Don't measure yourself by the standards of others. Be committed to measuring your worth by God's standard. His feelings about your physical appearance are already laid out in Scripture. You are the beautiful daughter of the King of kings. You are enough, and your beauty is the crown of creation.

But there are areas of our lives where He calls us to improve. When we remain close to Christ and abide in Him, the Holy Spirit will work in our lives to produce good results: "The fruit of the Spirit is love, joy, peace, patience, kindness, goodness, faithfulness, gentleness and self-control. Against such things there is no law" (Galatians 5:22–23).

Step 3: Get Filled Up

Turning our eyes to the standards of God and away from the people around us leads to contentment, and contentment comes from being filled up by the promises of God. My eyes can focus on the prize because I can embrace who I am in Christ. His Word makes it clear that He is madly in love with me. No standard of man can compare to this beautiful truth.

1. What parts of your beauty are you most tempted to compare to others? Who do you find yourself comparing your beauty to most often?

2. What have been the specific consequences of playing the comparison game in your life?

3. How can you begin to shift your thinking so that you use God's standard to measure your worth?

9

THE TROUBLE WITH BODY IMAGE:
ALTERED PERSPECTIVES AND FUN HOUSE MIRRORS

As I consider my own struggle with beauty and identity, I notice that, surprisingly, the seasons when that struggle was most intense were actually the seasons when I was the thinnest.

When I weighed fifty pounds less than I do now and wore a tiny size 4, I was the closest to the world's standard of beauty that I had ever been. I didn't see it that way, though. I would wake up every morning and stare into a mirror that I was sure was playing tricks on me. Others noticed I was slimming down, but I simply couldn't see it.

What I thought I saw when I looked at myself was not reality.

I know I'm not the only one to struggle with a distorted body image. Many of you struggle with the same false views of yourself. This distortion can have far-reaching effects.

What exactly is "body image"? It's more about your perception of yourself than about your actual size and shape. Body image includes how you see yourself when you look in the mirror or when you picture yourself in your mind. It is what you believe about your own appearance, including how you think others see you. In other words, body image describes how you feel about your body.

A healthy body image is a key element in our battle to accept God's words about our beauty. A distorted body image is often a foundational factor in many girls' struggle to embrace their beauty.

How can you know if your perceptions of yourself are accurate? What is the litmus test for deciding whether your body image is healthy? Let's take a couple of tests to see where you stand.

Get Out Your Crayons

Gather up some crayons or markers and a blank piece of paper. Find a place where you can concentrate. Take a few moments to draw a self-portrait. Be sure to include all of the major elements of your physical self. Do your best to draw your proportions the way that you see them. Will you be tall or short? Thick or thin? Think about the parts of your body that bother you and make sure that they make it into your drawing. Consider the components of your body that you like and be sure to include them too. Don't worry; you won't be graded on your artistic ability. The point of this assignment is simply to assess your body image.

Now take your drawing to a mirror. Does what you see in the mirror match what you just drew? Try to find a recent picture of yourself. Set it beside your drawing. Do your proportions look the same in the picture as they do in the image you drew? Is the photo version of you thinner or heavier than the crayon version?

Now try something a little scarier. Find someone you trust to shoot straight and ask them about the accuracy of your drawing. Choose someone who isn't in your peer group, because our friends tend to tell us what we want to hear. Find someone trustworthy who is a little older than you, such as a mentor, teacher, or even your mom.

What did they think? Did they confirm that your drawing was accurate or did they point out inconsistencies? Did they say that you drew yourself heavier than you really are, or taller, or that you exaggerated your flaws? If so, you may struggle with a distorted body image.

Quiz Time

Still convinced that your body image is accurate? Then you won't mind taking my body image quiz. Simply answer yes or no to the following questions.

- Do you compare your body to your friends and consistently "come up short"? Y_✓_ N____

- Is it difficult for you to look at your body in a full-length mirror? Y_✓_ N____

- Do you often wear baggy clothing specifically to hide your body? Y_✓_ N____

- Have you ever wanted to miss school or work because you were embarrassed about your body? Y_✓_ N____

- Do you avoid having your photo taken? Y_✓_ N____

- When you look at yourself in the mirror, do you spend a lot of time dwelling on flaws? Y_✓_ N____

- Do you avoid mirrors? Y____ N_✓_

- Do you feel uncomfortable when others compliment the way you look? Y_✓_ N____

- When you look at a fashion magazine, do you feel uncomfortable about your appearance? Y_✓_ N____

- Can you think of several people with whom you would trade bodies if possible? Y_✓_ N____

Did you answer yes to many of those questions? Maybe all of them? If so, it is likely that your body image is distorted. And I think that it is important for you to know that you are not alone. Many women look in the mirror and perceive a body that doesn't match their true figure. Many of us have fallen into the trap of exaggerating our flaws and nurturing a body image that is unhealthy.

Researchers have tested the pervasiveness of distorted body images among us. *Psychology Today* polled 4,000 readers in a body image survey. Of those surveyed, 56 percent of women and 43 percent of men reported that they were dissatisfied with their overall appearance. Of those who reported that they were satisfied overall, two-thirds of women and over half of the men stated that they were dissatisfied with their weight. Of those women surveyed, 89 percent reported that they wanted to lose weight. Only 3 percent said that they wanted to gain weight, and only 8 percent reported that they wanted their weight to stay the same.[1]

Well over half of young women report that they are dissatisfied with their bodies. However, experts estimate that only 15–20 percent of young women are actually overweight.[2] The conclusion is that large numbers of women are basing their dissatisfaction with the way they look on a perception of themselves that isn't accurate.

Researchers have proven that we distort our body image specifically by overestimating our weight. Research indicates that more than half of women overestimate the size of their bodies. A study at St. George's Hospital Medical School in London confirmed these results. When they asked a group of women to estimate the width of a box, fifty average-sized women were right on target. But when those same women were asked to estimate their own widths, they exaggerated the size of their waists by 25 percent and their hips by 16 percent.[3]

Where would you fit in these studies? Would you be among those women who are dissatisfied with their bodies even though they are healthy and normal? Would you overestimate the size of your waist? Would you have to admit to seeing yourself as heavier than you truly are? Would researchers report that you exaggerate your flaws or that your frustration with your appearance is not based on facts?

DO YOU EXAGGERATE YOUR FLAWS?

As if getting us to obsess over our bodies just the way they are isn't destructive enough, Satan often distorts our perception to the point that our body image becomes a misrepresentation of the truth. Does he ever whisper in your ear that you are the only woman in the world who struggles with body image? Do you let him convince you that you are bigger than you are? Once again, he demonstrates that when it comes to our beauty, he is the father of lies. And once again, God's truth proves that we are beautiful, treasured, and designed with exactly the bodies God intended us to have.

Let's take a look at four key truths about body image as part of our journey to unleash God's truth on this area of our lives.

Truth #1: The Body Image of the World Isn't Real

Our twisted body image is not without cause. We are inundated from every media outlet with images of bodies that look nothing like ours. The bodies that our society esteems as ideal are slimmer and more perfectly proportioned than ours will ever be.

The Body Shop ran an advertising campaign that announced, "There are three billion people who don't look like supermodels and only eight who do." And yet we strive to look like one of those eight! Our reflection doesn't look anything like the model on a magazine cover or commercial. Our skin isn't perfect. Our measurements don't match those we see on billboards. Our hair is occasionally out of place. And we are led to the conclusion that something is wrong with us. But as we explored in chapter 6, the body image that the world offers is a bold-faced lie. Every photo is airbrushed, Photoshopped, and altered so that very little remnant of realistic beauty is left. It is vital that you realize your beauty will never measure up to the standard of beauty offered by the world. This is no reflection on you, your body, or your beauty. The world's image of the body is a sham. Don't buy the lie.

Truth #2: A Misguided Body Image Can Have Far-Reaching Effects

Continuing to nurse a flawed body image can have disastrous consequences. Individuals with distorted body images are much more likely to struggle with eating disorders.[4] In addition, negative body image has been linked to low self-esteem, depression, sexual dysfunction, and poor health habits.[5]

I know from experience that this phenomenon can also have dramatic, negative effects on our relationships with others and on our walk with Christ. Can you think of some examples from your own life? Have you avoided relationships because you were embarrassed about the way you looked? Have you been so consumed with your body that you failed to nurture your spirit? Have others distanced themselves from you because they are confused by your false perception of self?

As we acknowledge that believing lies about our appearance can have lasting effects, we see why Satan sets this trap for so many of us. Continuing to believe lies in any area of our lives is dangerous. To do so in the area of our beauty can be devastating.

Truth #3: Your Body Image Is Part of Your Legacy

"I just didn't know that I would be passing on my feelings about my body to you girls," my mom said after yet another discussion turned to my struggle with weight. My sister Nikki and I both struggle with our body image, and while we take responsibility for our own insecurities, there is no denying that watching our mom struggle with her perception of herself played a huge role in shaping how we view ourselves.

A few days later I found myself having another familiar conversation.

"Please let me do it, Jason," I pleaded. "It won't hurt anyone." For about the billionth time, I was begging my husband, Jason, to let me have plastic surgery to remove the flaps of skin that cover the corners of my eyes. I was convinced that this minor procedure would greatly enhance my looks and solve every problem I ever had with my face.

Jason's answer stunned me.

"If that's what you want to do, go ahead, but I think it would have a dramatic effect on the women in your life," he said. "I think it would send a pretty clear message that you don't want to send."

He was right. And what he said applies to whatever part of your appearance you have allowed yourself to believe is accidental or a mistake. How you view yourself will be passed on to those around you. It will affect your friends. It will affect the friends you are trying to witness to. It will affect your ability to be salt and light in this dark world.

And someday, it will have a dramatic impact on your children.

For many of us, our body image is inherited, and in many families failure to accept ourselves the way that we are has become a generational sin. But what if *we* decided to be a generation of change? What if *we* were the women who rose up together to fight against the world's false image of beauty? What if *we* found the courage to look in the mirror with new eyes ready to see ourselves clearly and love what we see? What would *our* legacy become? Are you interested in joining me to find out?

Truth #4: A Distorted Body Image Misses the Mark and Requires You to Take Action

Throughout the chapters of this book, a pattern emerges. When Satan's lies about our beauty and worth have been exposed and replaced with truth, we have been increasingly free to embrace God's message that we are beautiful, lovely, and adored. The same is true in regard to our body image. Accepting a distorted body image is the same as believing a lie about ourselves. God calls us toward His truth and He calls us to see ourselves as He sees us and as we really are.

James 1:22–25 (TNIV) encourages us to do more than know God's truth. These verses challenge us to stand up and do something once we discover that we've been deceived. "Do not merely listen to the word, and so deceive yourselves. Do what it says. Those who listen to the word but do not do what it says are like people who look at their faces in a mirror and, after looking at themselves, go away and immediately forget what they look like. But those who look intently into the perfect law that gives freedom and continue in it—not forgetting what they have heard but doing it—they will be blessed in what they do."

This passage is exceptionally powerful when we apply it to our perceptions of our bodies. Scripture warns that if we listen to the Word and do nothing with it, we are like a person who forgets the reality of her own appearance. Isn't this exactly what many of us have done for years? We don't believe our own reflection. Instead we nurture a perception of ourselves that isn't based in fact. God's Word is a resounding reality check about the truth of our appearance. Our bodies were created in God's image and with purpose. Our size and shape are not hidden from God but are evidence of His creative genius and attention to the details of our existence. Despite our weight or shape, we are the handiwork of a loving God who pursues a relationship with us.

We are called to do more than walk away from these truths and forget them. Second Corinthians 10:5 tells us to "take captive every thought to make it obedient to Christ." This includes every thought about our bodies and appearance. Philippians 2:14 admonishes us to "Do everything without complaining or arguing." The word *everything* makes it clear that we are called to stop complaining about every area of our lives, including how we look. The final nail in the coffin of our obsession with our distorted body image can be found in 1 John 2:15 where we are told, "Do not love the world or anything in the world." This is especially true of the world's version of beauty. There is no room in our hearts to embrace the false body image that the world offers. Instead, we are called to fill our hearts with God's standard of beauty, a process that will naturally lead us to a healthier body image and perception of ourselves.

Go take a good hard look at yourself in the mirror. You're looking at the beautiful creation of a loving God. Allow the truth of your worth and beauty to begin to change what you see. Give yourself the freedom to admire yourself as the work of God's hand. Go ahead and smile. Drink deeply from the fountain of truth that you are beautiful just the way you are, and refuse to walk away and forget that God is calling you to embrace truth and abandon lies in the arena of your worth.

♡ JOURNAL PROMPTS

1. Is your body image accurate? In what specific ways have you misread your appearance?

2. What message does your perception of yourself send to others? What is your beauty legacy?

3. What actions can you take to move toward a healthier body image?

10

DISORDERED EATING:
FINDING BALANCE

My hunger to feel beautiful had physical side effects. It ultimately led to an eating disorder. I all but stopped eating. I overexercised. I found physical ways to act out the dissatisfaction I was feeling on the inside.

Maybe you have done the same. In our country alone, as many as ten million young women are fighting a life-threatening battle with an eating disorder such as anorexia or bulimia.[1] Experts report a rise in the incidence of anorexia in young women ages fifteen to nineteen every decade since 1930. The incidence of bulimia has tripled in the past 15 years.[2] Young women are literally dying to fit the beauty mold of our culture.

These statistics are alarming, but the disordered eating habits of most young women do not fit into the blanket categories of anorexics or bulimics. Would you be surprised to learn that almost all of us have developed some type of disordered eating habits? I'll describe several in this chapter.

I once heard food described as a tiger in a box. Keeping control of our eating habits is like keeping a tiger locked away. We take it out three times a day to feed it and then lock it away again until hunger strikes. A tiger is not easily controlled and is not likely to allow itself to be locked up without a fight. Food can be the same way. We are forced to interact with food several times a day, and yet our eating patterns can be difficult to control.

This is one more area of our lives that we can bring under the authority of Christ. We read in Galatians 5 that one of the fruits of the Spirit is self-control. This includes the practice of self-control in the way that we treat food.

And in chapter 11 we'll talk about being self-controlled and alert. Why? Because our "enemy the devil prowls around like a roaring lion looking for someone to devour" (1 Peter 5:8).

Self-control is an important spiritual discipline, and learning to practice self-control in the area of food is significant as we embrace God's authority in the area of our beauty. Recognizing our disordered eating patterns is a key first step to finding freedom in this area. I couldn't begin to find healing in the area of food until I admitted I had a problem. As less harmful disordered eating patterns have developed in my life over the years, I have needed to return to this first step of acknowledgment in order to begin the journey toward self-control.

Let's Do Lunch

I'd like to invite you out to lunch with a group of my friends. They are all healthy girls, but like you, they don't always recognize their own beauty, and as a result they've adopted some disordered eating patterns. Let me introduce you to them.

First, meet my friend Christy, the crash dieter. Christy eats well most of the time, but occasionally she freaks out about her beauty. Maybe someone makes a comment that causes her to question if she is thin enough. Maybe she passes a mirror that offers a reflection that is unflattering. Maybe she allows herself to play the comparison game. For whatever reason, she decides to react and starts to diet. One week she's on the Atkins diet. The next week she's trying to eat only fruits and vegetables. She rarely has much success in losing weight, but dieting gives her a sense of control for a while.

Christy is in good company. In a recent survey of college campuses, 91 percent of women reported that they had attempted to control their weight through dieting, and 22 percent dieted "often" or "always."[3] What Christy doesn't realize is that 35 percent of "normal dieters" progress to pathological dieters and of those, 20–25 percent develop eating disorders.[4]

Then there's Molly, the meal skipper. Just like Christy,

Molly is healthy. No one would accuse her of having an eating disorder, but occasionally she skips a meal or two. Sometimes she skips meals because she is feeling fat, and depriving herself of food makes her feel more in control. Sometimes she just gets busy and forgets to eat. Most of the time, she would rather spend her lunch break catching up with friends than preparing and eating a meal.

But Molly has forgotten that her body is a temple. By regularly skipping meals, she is depriving her body of what it needs. Just like Christy, Molly is putting herself at risk for developing an eating disorder. Over half of teenage girls and nearly one-third of teenage boys are like Molly—they use unhealthy weight control behaviors such as skipping meals, fasting, smoking cigarettes, vomiting, and taking laxatives to gain control over their food and their bodies.[5] The effect is often a downward spiral.

My eating disorder developed over a long period of time. First I cut out breakfast, then lunch. The more meals I skipped, the easier it got to keep skipping. I thought I was controlling my tiger in a box, but it wasn't long before it had me by the throat.

Maybe you've met someone like my next friend, Jessica, the junk-food junkie. Jessica doesn't put much thought into what makes it past her lips. Nutrition doesn't matter much to her, and she is a slave to her sweet tooth. Just like Molly, Jessica makes choices that deprive her body of what it needs, and she fails to treat it like the temple of the Most High God.

Olivia the Overeater and Stressed-out Susan have similar relationships with food. Both of them use food to soothe them when life feels hectic and out of control. Olivia fills the voids in her heart with too much food. If she feels emotionally or spiritually empty, she makes sure that she is physically stuffed. She is among a growing population of individuals who have become overweight because they can't control their eating patterns. Susan looks fit as a fiddle, but catch her on the day of a big test or a relationship crisis and you'll find her dipping deep into a tub of Rocky Road. Food has become her coping mechanism. Instead of casting her cares onto Christ, she has developed a tendency to seek the counsel of Ben and Jerry.

Where would you fit in at this table? Can you identify with one or more of these disordered eating patterns? Is this an area of your life where you need to invite Christ to retrain your thoughts and actions? Has food become a wild animal that is difficult for you to control or an area of your life that you try to overcontrol when the rest of your world starts spinning?

Christ cares about every nook and cranny of your life. His words offer guidance for daily living, and we can find many Scriptures devoted to the topic of food. Isn't it interesting that the original sin centered around food (remember the fruit of the Tree of Knowledge of Good and Evil?) or that Christ's first miracle was food-and-drink related (when He changed water into wine at a wedding)? Before He was arrested Christ shared one last meal with His friends, and He used that evening to encourage us to use food as a reminder of His sacrifice through Communion. And when Christ reminds His followers in Revelation 3:20 of the intimate relationship He desires to have with us, He talks about dining together: "If anyone hears my voice and opens the door, I will come in and eat with him, and he with me."

Food Is God's Provision

When God called the Israelites out of slavery in Egypt, He agreed to meet their every need. One of His many miracles of provision came in the form of manna from heaven. During that season of journeying, His people did not have to hunt or gather; the Lord provided all of the food that their bodies needed (Exodus 16:14–18). He provides for our physical needs in ways that are no less miraculous and consistent. It is easy for us to forget that God is our provider when we can easily go to the grocery store or a drive-thru anytime hunger strikes. But God is the One who created our food sources. He is the Maker and Sustainer of all life. Psalm 104:14 states that "he makes grass grow for the cattle and plants for man to cultivate—bringing forth food from the earth." And "he provides food for the those who fear him; he remembers his covenant forever" (Psalm 111:5). Psalm 136 reminds us that we serve a good God and that He is the provider of food for all of His creatures. He *"gives food to every creature.* His love endures forever. Give thanks to the God of heaven. His love endures forever" (vv. 25–26).

God's provision of food for each of us is an expression of His love. "The Lord is faithful to all his promises and loving toward all he has made. . . . You give them their food at the proper time. You open your hand and satisfy the desires of every living thing," we read in Psalm 145:13, 15–16. The author of Ecclesiastes reminds us that every good gift comes from God's hand, including food and drink. "People can do nothing better than to eat and drink and find satisfaction in their toil. This too, I see, is from the hand of God, for without him, who can eat or find enjoyment?" (2:24–25 TNIV).

Sometimes we develop spiritual eating disorders. We binge and purge on Jesus or fast from Him altogether and our souls quickly become malnourished. Matthew 5:6 says, "Blessed are those who hunger and thirst for righteousness, for they will be filled." Do you hunger for Jesus? Are you thirsty for the touch of His hand on your life? Or have you developed a spiritual eating disorder? Let's do a quick checkup.

Spiritual bulimia

Do you binge on Jesus? Do you get filled up at camp or weekend retreats or on Sunday morning and then purge so that you can live the life you want to live? Instead of getting a steady dose of Christ through His Word, do you count on filling feasts of God every once in a while?

(continued on next page . . .)

(continued from page 115 . . .)

Read Matthew 13:5–6 and see
if you are like the shallow soil.
Without the constant nourishment
of consistent time in the Word and
fellowship with other believers,
your heart will get sick.

Spiritual anorexia

Do you starve yourself of
Jesus altogether? Do you go weeks
and months without seeking Him
in prayer, fellowshipping with
other Christians, or digging into
the Word? It is impossible for
your spirit to stay healthy when
it is cut off from the source of life
and strength. Anorexics delude
themselves by thinking they can
avoid food and still stay healthy,
but it doesn't work that way.

In the same way, you cannot
grow spiritually without the
nutrients God offers.

In Colossians 1:9–11 Paul
writes, "For this reason, since
the day we heard about you, we
have not stopped praying for
you and asking God to fill you
with the knowledge of his will
through all spiritual wisdom and
understanding. And we pray this
in order that you may live a life
worthy of the Lord and please
him in every way: bearing fruit
in every good work, growing
in the knowledge of God, being
strengthened with all power
according to his glorious might."

Growth and strength come
from being filled by God. Don't
starve yourself of His teachings.
Feast regularly. Get filled up. It is
simply the only way to grow in Him.

Spiritual stress eating

Are you a crisis pray-er who
runs to Jesus only when the going
gets tough? Do you neglect Him
when life is smooth but seek Him
with urgency when the road
gets rocky? He is certainly able
to provide for us during times of
trial. Nahum 1:7 promises, "The
Lord is good, a refuge in times of
trouble. He cares for those who
trust in him." But He calls us to
seek Him at all times, not just
when troubles hit our lives. First
Thessalonians 5:16–18 teaches us to
"be joyful always; pray continually;
give thanks in all circumstances,
for this is God's will for you in
Christ Jesus." Did you catch it?
Always . . . continually . . . in all
circumstances. We are to ingest a
steady diet of Christ, rather than
just running to Him when we are
stressed and afraid.

Do a spiritual checkup. If your
spiritual life has developed some
disordered eating habits, pull up a
chair and feast at the banquet table
of God. Allow Him to fill you and
nourish your heart.

Jesus consistently provided food for those in need during His earthly ministry. Many people are familiar with the time Jesus miraculously provided for over five thousand hungry followers using just five loaves of bread and two fish (Matthew 14:13–21). Later He had compassion on a crowd of more than four thousand and turned seven loaves and a few fish into an abundant feast (Matthew 15:32–37). One time Jesus astonished His disciples by providing such a catch of fish that the nets they used began to break (Luke 5:1–11). He did something similar as recorded in John 21:1–13. This time 153 fish were ensnared. Peter was so excited that he jumped right into the water before the catch could even be counted! Jesus completed the miracle, staying for breakfast with His friends.

Our God is willing and able to provide for our physical needs. All that we have is a gift from His hand. As part of retraining our thoughts and behaviors in the area of food, we must realize that our food is provided by our heavenly Father as evidence of His great love for us.

Food Is Good

In our world of carb- and calorie-consciousness, it is easy to believe that food is an enemy. The media teaches us to feel guilty about food while simultaneously driving us toward food choices that are unwise. We are supposed to limit carbohydrates, eat five fruits and vegetables a day, and drink at least eight glasses of water; and if we do not, we are shamed into vowing to do better tomorrow or next week or next year. But does the Bible echo these sentiments?

Ecclesiastes 9:7 makes it clear that food is good and gives us permission to enjoy it. "Go, eat your food with gladness, and drink your wine with a joyful heart, for it is now that God favors what you do." In the New Testament, Jesus tells us, "What goes into a man's mouth does not make him 'unclean,' but what comes out of his mouth, that is what makes him 'unclean'" (Matthew 15:10). The early church in Rome got so wrapped up in defining which foods were good and which foods were bad that Paul was forced to address it in a letter to them. He said, "As one who is in the Lord Jesus, I am fully convinced that no food is unclean in itself" (Romans 14:14). He goes on to encourage them not to quarrel about something as minor as food. "Do not destroy the work of God for the sake of food" (v. 20).

Food Is Not Intended to Be a Source of Worry

Food is God's provision, and as such, food is good. It seems like a waste of time and energy to allow ourselves to feel guilty and frustrated because of food. This is not to say that we have free rein to eat whatever we want. Ultimately we must remember to treat our bodies as temples. But Scripture does give us permission to enjoy food and reminds us that what goes into our mouth isn't nearly as significant as what we allow to come out of our lips.

If God is willing and able to provide all the food that we need and if He declares that food is good, why should we allow it to be a source of worry or anxiety? There is freedom in Christ. He hammers this point home in Matthew 6:25–27.

"Therefore I tell you, do not worry about your life, what you will eat or drink; or about your body, what you will wear. Is not life more important than food, and the body more important than clothes? Look at the birds of the air; they do not sow or reap or store away in barns, and yet your heavenly Father feeds them. Are you not much more valuable than they? Who of you by worrying can add a single hour to his life?"

I'll tell you what I did not know when I was trapped by an eating disorder: I was a slave to food. My thoughts were controlled with guilt and fear, and my actions were unhealthy, unsatisfying, and out of order. All of the characters I mentioned earlier struggle with the same feelings of shame and frustration from time to time. But freedom *can* be found. Run to Christ when you're feeling fat and frumpy. Let Him fill you with the truth of His love and His admiration for your beauty. Seek Him when you are feeling stressed. Allow Him to be your Prince of Peace instead of seeking solace in snacks. Allow the truth that you are a temple to penetrate your heart deeply. Let that miraculous thought change how you see yourself and how you nourish your body and spirit.

Today I am free from the claws of my tiger in a box. Tomorrow I might struggle again. But I know where to run for answers. Christ is able to tame all the wild animals in my heart and life, and He is doing so day by day as I seek Him and chase after His design for my life. It is my prayer that you will allow Him to do the same for you.

♡ JOURNAL PROMPTS

1. Can you identify any of your disordered eating patterns?

2. Is food often a source of worry for you? In what specific ways does food cause you anxiety?

3. Are there specific eating patterns that you need to reform? How can you begin that process?

I HATE EATING DISORDERS.

11

TAKING AIM AT YOUR ENEMY:
EXPLORING THE SPIRITUAL SIDE OF OUR PHYSICAL STRUGGLE

My roommate in college was a knockout. I mean a magazine cover–worthy beauty. She had long, curly, dark hair, clear skin, and a figure that was unfairly fabulous. She was naturally thin, but not scrawny. And without much effort on her part, she was graced with toned abs and firm arms.

I distinctly remember one afternoon dashing in from my step aerobics class in my baggy T-shirt with my face bright red from exertion and my hair sticking out in about a million directions only to find her lounging around in front of the TV, eating junk food, looking cool and fabulous. She was (and still is) a natural beauty.

You would think that with natural beauty would come natural confidence. Not so. My roommate made faces in the mirror just as often as I did and, through many conversations over Andy's Frozen Custard, I discovered a great mystery. My naturally beautiful, effortlessly thin roomie questioned her own worth and beauty as if she was unaware of how stunning she was. She helped me begin to realize an important truth about my own identity—and yours too. Could it be that the source of this struggle has nothing to do with the reality of our appearance? If truly beautiful women, like my roommate, don't feel comfortable in their own skin, is it possible that the root of this issue is internal?

I know other women who would not fit into the world's beauty mold. They would never be asked to appear on the cover of a fashion magazine, but they carry them-selves well and exude a confident spirit. They confirm the lesson that my roommate originally taught me: Whether or not we measure up to the world's standard of attractiveness, the core of our beauty issues are rooted in the heart.

On journal pages written long ago, I wrote about my feelings of worthlessness. I didn't know it at the time, but I was also hinting at a connection between those feelings and my relationship with my Savior.

DECEMBER 21, 1997
I FIND MYSELF SAYING AND TRULY BELIEVING THAT I AM WORTHLESS AND STUPID. WHAT HAPPENED TO MAKE ME SEE MYSELF AS WORTHLESS? I KNOW GOD IS DISAPPOINTED.

Not long after, I wrote about the consequences of failing to understand my worth.

JANUARY 3, 1998
SPIRITUALLY, I AM DRY AS A DESERT. I PRAY THAT GOD WILL SEE MY WEAKNESS AND SOON BRING RAIN.

Looking back, I can see the clear connection between my feelings of worthlessness and my dried-up spirit. I looked in the mirror and saw flaws, and I felt that some distance was creeping between me and Jesus.

As I speak to young women across the country, I've discovered that I am not alone. There is a pattern. When women fail to tap into the source of true beauty, when we find our worth in worldly standards (a cheap substitute, by the way), when we compare ourselves to others, when we find our identity in boys, and in clothes and designer handbags, then the sacred is torn. There are spiritual consequences for our struggle with our physical appearance.

Amber Kay Bowen, a twenty-year-old college student, writes this:

"My battle with self-image started when I was in elementary school, before I had the abundant life that only Jesus can bring. I was never the cute, athletic, skinny girl everyone admired.

I was the short chubby girl who often got overlooked. My self-esteem was basically nonexistent. When I got into middle school, I thought things would get better, but I was wrong. Things only got worse, with older students making belittling comments about me. Finally, I had had enough. I decided after my sixth grade year that I would get in shape over the summer and blow people away when I came back for seventh grade.

"I started out by just working out more, but it slowly became an obsession. I felt like I had to work out after every time I ate anything. I remember very clearly that one time after I ate a Jolly Rancher I felt like I had to go run a mile because I had just consumed too many calories. It got to the point that I began cutting certain things out of my diet altogether, starting with soda, which seemed to be a logical choice to start with. Then cake was gone, all desserts, bacon, any fried food, until eventually I was eating lettuce and carrots. The only reason I even ate at all was because I had to—my parents made me.

"My whole family was going through a hard time that summer because a tornado had destroyed our house. We were all stressed out anyway, so it was really easy to hide my secret obsession behind the stress of the summer and the

inability to eat well when we were living in a hotel for a month. No one, not even myself, noticed how badly I was hurting myself until I had already taken it too far. I liked it when no one noticed, when I could do my own thing without drawing attention to myself. I liked being overlooked.

"After our house was rebuilt and we moved back in, things started getting back to normal. Everyone at school noticed that I had lost a lot of weight, and I loved the attention. I thought I was gorgeous simply because I was thin. I went from a size 14 at the beginning of that summer to a size 3 by the end. I was so excited. When the newness of my appearance wore off, I felt worthless. I felt like no one noticed me anymore, and I was just the overlooked girl again."

When I think about my beautiful friend Amber and the fact that for even a moment she would doubt her beauty and worth, I get angry—not at Amber, but at her Enemy. Amber's story reminds me that we have an Enemy who is relentless in his quest to turn the gifts of God (including our beauty) into ugliness. What I want you to begin to understand is that your struggle with body image, esteem, and identity is spiritual, not physical. It is important to realize that you have an Enemy who seeks to rob you of your beauty and who lies to you about your worth. Together we'll explore the spiritual realm and develop strategies to win against the Evil One.

Know Your Enemy

The Bible reminds us who our Enemy is and encourages us to study his tactics.

"For our struggle is not against flesh and blood, but against the rulers, against the authorities, against the powers of this dark world and against the spiritual forces of evil in the heavenly realms" (Ephesians 6:12).

What? Culture is not to blame? Fashion magazines and supermodels aren't the source of our insecurity? No, not according to God's Word. When you begin to question your very value, you are indeed engaged in battle, but it is with an Enemy who has his sights set on your destruction. Scripture also warns us that the Devil isn't passive. He diligently seeks to take what God intends for good and turn it into darkness.

"Be self-controlled and alert. Your enemy the devil prowls around like a roaring lion looking for someone to devour" (1 Peter 5:8).

Your Enemy is not a jovial guy in a cheap red cape. He doesn't just stretch the truth. He lies to you about your worth—bold, terrible lies—and he is actively seeking to convince you that you are anything less than the stunning daughter of the King of kings.

Knowing that, it is your job to study him, to learn his tactics, and to put on the full armor of God so that you can win the fight.

My brother is a soldier in the U. S. Army. He spent a year fighting in Iraq. But the military didn't just give him boots and ship him overseas. He had to train—hard. He spent months learning about his enemy's tactics. He learned what weapons they might use, what his enemies look like, and when they were likely to attack. He endured grueling physical training in preparation for battle. He trained for the worst while the rest of us prayed for the best. Why? Because in order to fight against an enemy, you must know your enemy; otherwise, you are a sitting duck, begging for a surprise attack.

The same is true for us.

We must be alert, "in order that Satan might not outwit us. For we are not unaware of his schemes" (2 Corinthians 2:11).

No Stranger to Beauty

Satan might be caricatured as a disgusting creature with warts, scaly skin, and flaming nostrils, but in 2 Corinthians 11:14, Paul warns us that Satan "masquerades as an angel of light." And hundreds of years before Paul, Ezekiel described him as a creature of awe-inspiring beauty.

 . . . You were the model of perfection, full of wisdom and perfect in beauty. You were in Eden, the garden of God; every precious stone adorned you: ruby, topaz and emerald, chrysolite, onyx and jasper, sapphire, turquoise and beryl. Your settings and mountings were made of gold; on the day you were created they were prepared . . . (Ezekiel 28:12–13)

At first glance, it seems like the author of this passage must be describing Michael or Gabriel or any of the other beautiful celestial beings set apart to do God's will. But as the writer continues, we notice that this being's beauty has become his downfall. His splendor has led to rebellion.

 . . . You were filled with violence, and you sinned. So I drove you in disgrace from the mount of God, and I expelled you, O guardian cherub, from among the fiery stones. Your heart became proud on account of your beauty, and you corrupted your wisdom because of your splendor. (Ezekiel 28:16–17)

This passage was written to the king of Tyre, but references to the garden of Eden indicate that the author is addressing our Enemy, Satan. Notice that the writer does not describe Satan as hideous, repulsive, or even mildly unattractive. Quite the opposite—he is "the model of perfection," "perfect in beauty," and adorned with precious stones.

Satan knows what beauty is, but, true to his character, he is bent on destruction. He seeks to take God-given beauty and disfigure it. He has been distorting our view of beauty and worth successfully from the very beginning.

It Started in the Garden

I have no doubt that Eve was beautiful. She is the birth of femininity. Her form was created by the very breath of God and to top it all off, she was the only woman in creation. There were no supermodels or midriff-bearing pop princesses to compare her to (though I am convinced that they wouldn't have measured up).

Satan recognized her beauty and he slithered in to undo God's good work.

"'You will not surely die [if you eat the fruit of the tree],' the serpent said to the woman. 'For God knows that when you eat of it your eyes will be opened, and you will be like God, knowing good and evil.'

"When the woman saw that the fruit of the tree was good for food and pleasing to the eye, and also desirable for gaining wisdom, she took some and ate it. She also gave some to her husband, who was with her, and he ate it. Then the eyes of both of them were opened, and they realized they were naked; so they sewed fig leaves together and made coverings for themselves" (Genesis 3:4–7).

And just like that, with one big lie, followed by one little bite, Eve became ashamed of her beauty. She rushed to cover up what God had made, and among the other things we inherited that go with a sin nature is the struggle to accept our worth. Satan lied to Eve in the garden, and he has continued to lie to women ever since.

Lies Satan Tells (and We Believe)

If Satan is anything, he is a liar. The Bible calls him the father of lies (John 8:44). As part of our battle plan, we need to recognize the unholy lies Satan often tells us about our worth.

Lie #1: Your Worth Comes from Your Appearance

The billion-dollar fashion, beauty, and advertising industries are banking on you falling for this one.

My ritual when I fly is always the same. I wear my favorite comfy black sweatshirt, buy a huge caramel latte to sip while I wait, and spend way too much money at the magazine kiosk buying the most recent issues of my favorite magazines. On a trip to Wisconsin I had an unusually long layover, so I dug deep into my bank account to purchase not one, not two, but six magazines. As I scanned the covers, I found the same lies printed again and again.

One magazine promised to show me "77 ways to be more gorgeous," while also teaching me about the "Beauty Diet" and the secrets to "clear, glowing skin." I devoured this magazine from cover to cover even before my caramel latte had cooled down enough to drink. When I got home, I tried about 76 of the 77 beauty tips. No one seemed to notice the "more gorgeous" new me. I opted not to try the beauty diet since it encouraged the consumption of sardines, oysters, and sweet potatoes . . . ew!

Another magazine sported a teaser on its cover that said, "If you're over 26 read this! The new beauty breakthroughs that keep you young." Now I am indeed over 26, and as I stared at that cover I wondered when 26 had become the start date for anti-aging panic. But even while I reminded myself that I didn't need any beauty breakthrough help, I was adding the magazine to my stack.

As I read my twenty-three-dollars' worth of glossy print, some familiar feelings began to creep into my heart. I started to wonder why I didn't look like the girls on the covers of those magazines, and I began to feel pretty discouraged about my skin, hair, and jean size. But there was hope—see, if I could just manage to do everything these magazines suggested, I could be beautiful and as a result, happy!

But here's the problem: It was all a lie and I was believing it. Sure, I have some days when I fit into my skinny jeans and my hair decides to cooperate and I manage to put on eyeliner without looking like a member of an eighties rock band.

But it doesn't change my heart.

God's Word is clear. Your worth does not come from your appearance. See what He Himself says:

> . . . The Lord does not look at the things man looks at. Man looks at the outward appearance, but the Lord looks at the heart . . . (1 Samuel 16:7)
>
> Your beauty should not come from outward adornment, such as braided hair and the wearing of gold jewelry and fine clothes. Instead, it should be that of your inner self, the unfading beauty of a gentle and quiet spirit, which is of great worth in God's sight. (1 Peter 3:3–4)

Graffiti

Charm is deceptive, and beauty is fleeting; but a woman who fears the Lord is to be praised. (Proverbs 31:30)

Lie #2: Your Worth Comes from What You Do

I struggle with this one. I am always trying to be good enough, smart enough, and important enough to earn my significance. I find it very difficult not to base my feelings of worth on what I have managed to accomplish that day. In our achievement-obsessed culture, I bet you are feeling the pressure to go and to do and to be, just as much as I am.

This particular lie can have devastating effects on our spirit. If we are constantly trying to prove our worth by doing, we lose the freedom to just be ourselves. Am I accomplishing great things if I spend an afternoon staring out at the ocean? No. But I am nurturing inner beauty by connecting with God's creation and practicing the discipline of being still. Will I earn a trophy for spending a Saturday afternoon in my pj's rather than rushing to soccer practice, working on algebra homework, and practicing my clarinet? Nope. But I am certainly more beautiful when I cultivate inner peace and seek much-needed rest.

You have inherent worth because you are a child of God. He loves you and chose you, not because of what you could accomplish for Him or because He was impressed by your athletic, academic, or musical ability. He desires a relationship with you because you are the created and He is the Creator. There is nothing you could ever do to earn His favor and nothing you could ever do to make Him change His mind about you.

The Message puts it this way:

 You're blessed when you're content with just who you are—no more, no less. That's the moment you find yourselves proud owners of everything that can't be bought. (Matthew 5:5)

A young woman who understands her value in Christ will seek to do good in the world. She will serve others and, serving in the name of Christ, she can accomplish great things. But even so, true value cannot be defined by what we do, no matter how great our achievements are. A beautiful daughter of the King can rest in knowing that her worth is not dependent on what she can accomplish on her own.

Lie #3: Your Worth Is Determined by What Others Think of You

When I was in junior high, we had these awful things called slam books.

Everyone from my group of friends would write comments in each other's books. It was gut-wrenching. Because it was anonymous, people felt free to write whatever they wanted, and in the spirit of junior high drama at its best—surprise!— more comments were negative and cutting than positive and encouraging. I remember reading remarks that my friends had written and feeling my heart sink. People called me a snob and a flirt. Someone wrote, in bright purple ink to top it off, that I was ugly. Deep down, I knew those things weren't true, but they left bruises on my heart.

After a time the school authorities banned slam books. I guess they got tired of watching junior high girls burst into tears over words written in purple ink. I still have memories of insults from my peers, though. The old adage "sticks and stones may break my bones, but words will never hurt me" couldn't be further from the truth. The opinions of others can have a powerful impact on our feelings of worth.

However, basing your sense of worth on the perceptions of others is dangerous ground. Living your life for the accolades of people is like building your house on shifting sand. I have no doubt that you have learned by now how to win the praise of others. But if you cannot define your worth apart from what others think of you—if you are constantly looking to others for validation—if you need others to fill the voids of your heart and answer your questions about who you are—then you will find yourself desperately empty.

The lie Satan tells is that we must define our worth by what others think of us. The opinions of people are not necessarily factual, but are often based on perceptions that have nothing to do with who we really are or what we are really like. On top of that, perceptions are always changing. My first impressions of people are often wrong, and more than once someone I thought I knew and understood turned out to be someone else entirely. Another's opinion is not the measuring stick by which we can determine our value—Jesus is the source of your worth.

The Bible is rich with beautiful descriptions of God's love for you. I can't even come close to describing all of the affirmations of worth that Scripture offers to each of us. Jesus Himself revealed amazing truths about who we are during His short ministry. A look at the first gospel alone provides a compelling framework for who we are.

Jesus called you the "salt of the earth" and the "light of the world" in Matthew 5:13–14. That's high praise. In the next chapter He says plainly how valuable you are, while promising to take care of your every need (Matthew 6:26). He calls you a member of His family (Matthew 12:48–50) and, more specifically, you are His child (Matthew 7:9–11). I doubt that anyone else can offer you praise more powerful than the fact that you are acknowledged as the daughter of the King of kings. Jesus also reminds us that we are known fully by Him, even down to the number of hairs on our head (Matthew 10:30).

There is power in the realization that Jesus desires to know us and pursues intimacy with us. In the parable of the sheep, Jesus says again that we are worth pursuing, and by His death on the cross He demonstrates that we are worth dying for (Matthew 27:50).

After His resurrection He returns to His followers to remind them and us that we are His messengers, entrusted with the story of His saving grace. The first gospel is brought to a close with the reminder that we are never abandoned (Matthew 28:20).

God's Word has much to say about who you are. These truths are to be the rock on which you can build your sense of worth.

♡ JOURNAL PROMPTS

1. In what ways has your struggle to embrace your physical beauty had spiritual side effects?

2. It is important to know your Enemy. Can you identify specific tactics that Satan has used to convince you that your beauty is flawed? What are they?

3. Which of Satan's lies identified in this chapter are you most prone to believing? What truths can you find in Scripture to counteract these lies?

12

GOD'S VIEW OF BEAUTY:
FINDING HOPE IN THE WORD

As the Lord began to teach me that the world's standard of beauty was a scam, and as I began to realize the lies I had believed in the areas of identity and worth, I started to wonder if true beauty exists. I realized that my attempts to obtain the beauty standards of the people around me were hollow, but the longing to be beautiful remained. As much as I worked to try to convince myself that beauty didn't matter, I could not. The core of my feminine soul longed for beauty and ached for that beauty to be found in me.

I recognized that the Enemy had lied to me by convincing me that true beauty came from my outward appearance, but I could not shake the feeling that both my inward and outward beauty mattered a great deal. I wondered . . . if the world's standard of beauty isn't real, what is? If beauty can't be achieved by workouts, haircuts, and flattering clothes, how could true beauty be attained? What does God-given, God-pleasing beauty look like? Why do our hearts long for beauty? Why do we suspect that our beauty is one of the most powerful gifts we can give?

I realized that the world's view of beauty is a cheap substitute for a kind of beauty that only God can create within us—beauty that we were designed to showcase. Stories told throughout the Old and New Testaments reveal that God cares about beauty and that He even allows us to reveal it, but His ideals don't match the world's. They are the secret to beauty that lasts, fulfills, and transforms.

John and Stasi Eldredge, the authors of *Captivating*, one of my favorite books, assert that all women have a beauty to unveil. Instead of minimizing the importance of beauty, they write that beauty is essential.

> Beauty is transcendent. It is our most immediate experience of the eternal.
> Think of what it's like to behold a gorgeous sunset, or the ocean at dawn.
> Remember the ending of a great story. We yearn to linger, to experience it all our days. Sometimes the beauty is so deep it pierces us with longing. For what? For life as it was meant to be. Beauty reminds us of an Eden we have never known, but somehow know our hearts were created for. Beauty speaks of heaven to come, when all shall be beautiful. . . . Beauty draws us to God.

And then the authors reach a conclusion that Scripture makes obvious. Beauty is not reserved for sunsets and seashores. True beauty is most powerful when it is revealed by you.

> All of these things are true for any experience of Beauty. But they are especially true when we experience the beauty of a woman—her eyes, her form, her voice, her heart, her spirit, her life . . . she is beauty through and through.[1]

God's standard of beauty is awe-inspiring. You can attain it, and you were meant to reveal it. To embrace your worth from God's perspective is not the same as deciding that beauty, *both* inward and outward, doesn't matter. More accurately, it is a decision to build your value on the Rock instead of the shifting sands; that is, to build your value on the stable foundation of God's Word instead of the constantly changing standards of beauty offered by the world.

Outward Beauty Should be Matched by Inward Grace

Do you know someone who is beautiful on the outside, but the better you get to know her the less attractive she becomes? Can you think of someone famous who looks great in magazines, but whose life seems hollow and empty? Have you ever met someone who was so selfish or sarcastic or shallow that the outer appearance was eclipsed by a lack of inner beauty? Me too. So did Jesus.

Jesus often addressed the Pharisees of His day. These were the men who were doing everything right according to their religious law, and they looked great from the outside. They wore what they were supposed to wear. They cut their hair and trimmed their beards the way they were supposed to. They were invited to all the important parties. Based on appearances alone, they seemed to have their act together.

But Jesus saw their hearts, and He pointed out an important truth we can relate to our beauty. He was angry with the Pharisees, not because they did everything according to the law, but because their outward appearance was not matched with inward grace. He has the same standard for you and me.

In Matthew 23 Jesus' words reveal much about His view of beauty. "Woe to you, teachers of the law and Pharisees, you hypocrites! You clean the outside of the cup and dish, but inside they are full of greed and self-indulgence. Blind Pharisee! First clean the inside of the cup and dish, and then the outside also will be clean" (vv. 25–26).

I collect teacups. They are a physical reminder that I am precious, like fine china. One of my favorites was a gift from my grandma. It is delicate and beautiful, and my great-grandma used it at tea parties with her friends.

I have another teacup from a retreat I went to as a teenager. It was at that retreat that I made a commitment to remain pure until my wedding day. It has beautiful pink, tiny roses on it, and it is a precious reminder of that promise and of God's blessings on my life as a result.

One of my favorites came from my husband's great-great-grandfather. It has a garden of blue flowers painted on the front and gold letters too worn to read. These teacups are beautiful on the outside. But look closely and you'll realize that I haven't dusted in a while. They are dirty. Jesus described the Pharisees the same way. They may have looked flawless on the outside, but their hearts were ugly and unclean. Jesus demonstrated His distaste for this kind of beauty. But He offers hope. After reprimanding the Pharisees for their hollow beauty, He tells them to clean the inside of the cup first, and then the outside will be clean. A beautiful heart can't help but overflow to make us more beautiful on the outside.

Jesus told the analogy in even more graphic terms in verse 27:

> Woe to you, teachers of the law and Pharisees, you hypocrites! You are like whitewashed tombs, which look beautiful on the outside but on the inside are full of dead men's bones and everything unclean. (Matthew 23:27)

When Jesus begins a thought with the phrase "woe to you" it is His way of saying "listen up" and "I mean business." Our antennas should perk up when we read those words. Jesus means business when He speaks to the Pharisees this way, and He means business when He communicates the truth about His beauty standards for us.

Just like the cup, Jesus accuses the Pharisees of being something that appears beautiful to others but is cheapened by the fact that their hearts are in the wrong place. He doesn't dance around the subject, just suggesting that maybe they might want to work on their inner beauty. He doesn't merely point out that their hearts could use some tweaking. No, He bluntly compares the state of their spirits to dead men's bones and everything unclean. There is nothing pretty about death and nothing attractive about a body laid in the grave. Decay is inevitable. Anything outward is guaranteed to rot away.

It is easy for us to look down on the Pharisees. I find myself saying, "Amen, Jesus! Stick it to 'em!" as I read those words. But the reality is that sometimes I too am a whitewashed tomb. I bet there are days when you are also. You look fine on the outside. Your hair is fixed. Your makeup is applied. Your clothes are cute. But woe to you, because your heart is beginning to stink. No beauty has meaning apart from a humble heart. God's beauty standard above all else is that outward beauty, though important, must be matched with inward grace.

The Lord Looks upon the Heart

One of the most revealing passages regarding God's view of beauty can be found in 1 Samuel 16:1–13. This is one of my favorite stories in Scripture, and it has a lot to say about what God desires from each of us.

The story begins with the prophet Samuel mourning King Saul. Saul is the king of Israel, but because he has rejected God's commandments, the Lord has rejected him. Samuel mourns for his lost king and for the state of his country, but God springs into action. He commands Samuel to go to the house of Jesse to anoint a new king. Samuel argues with God, but eventually agrees and heads off to Jesse's house.

When he arrives, Samuel asks to see Jesse's sons. The oldest son comes into the room to greet Samuel. He is handsome and strong, but the Lord tells Samuel that he will not be king.

Then the Lord speaks the most amazing words. He says,

"Do not consider his appearance or his height, for I have rejected him. The Lord does not look at the things man looks at. Man looks at the outward appearance, but the Lord looks at the heart" (1 Samuel 16:7).

I find this to be a scary truth. As much as I struggle to accept my outward appearance as lovely, I know that my appearance is usually in better shape than my heart. I am prone to wander, prone to fear, prone to worry and doubt and discouragement. And that is where God is looking for my beauty? How can that be?

As the story continues, I find hope. One after another, Jesse presents his sons to Samuel, and to each one the Lord says no. In fact, Jesse had seven of his sons pass before Samuel and the Lord rejected each of them. Finally, with a sigh of desperation, Samuel asks, "Are these all the sons you have?" (v.11).

Jesse admits that he does have one more son. His name is David. Jesse hadn't even considered his youngest boy enough to bother bringing him in from the fields. But at Samuel's request, Jesse sends for David and he comes before the prophet.

"Then the Lord said, 'Rise and anoint him; he is the one'" (1 Samuel 16:12).

I love the underdog theme of this story. I love that his father Jesse missed the vision for David's life by thinking he was destined for shepherding, but that God's call was relentless and hard to ignore. And I love that the God I serve does not look at the things man looks at. I love that He does not consider my outer appearance. And that when He searches for beauty within my heart, He isn't looking for perfection, but delights in finding the tiny treasures of my love for Him.

David's heart was far from perfect. He wrote about his fear (Psalm 3), his exhaustion (Psalm 6), his guilt (Psalm 7), and his doubt (Psalm 13). David was a man who sinned, and like me, his heart was prone to wander. But the Lord found beauty there. Not because David's heart was perfect, but because it overflowed with love for God despite David's struggle with his flesh.

Bald Women

God's first beauty standard is that outward beauty should be matched with inward grace. He also shows us that He doesn't look at the things man looks at. He is searching for our beauty within the depths of our heart. And as we will discover in the book of Isaiah, God asks us to apply His beauty standards and to find our worth in things that last.

I love the story of the women of Zion found in Isaiah 3:16–26. At first glance, it sounds humorous, but a closer look reveals that these verses are a warning to those who chase the beauty standards of the world instead of the standards of God.

The premise of these passages is this: The women of Zion started to misuse their beauty, beauty that God had given them as a gift. Scripture records that they were haughty and flirtatious. Even the way they walked was meant to draw attention. God was displeased with their misuse of beauty, and so He took it away.

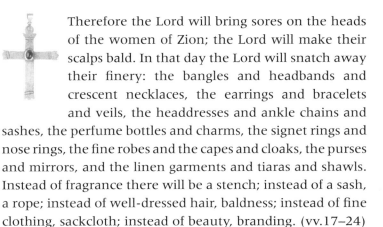 Therefore the Lord will bring sores on the heads of the women of Zion; the Lord will make their scalps bald. In that day the Lord will snatch away their finery: the bangles and headbands and crescent necklaces, the earrings and bracelets and veils, the headdresses and ankle chains and sashes, the perfume bottles and charms, the signet rings and nose rings, the fine robes and the capes and cloaks, the purses and mirrors, and the linen garments and tiaras and shawls. Instead of fragrance there will be a stench; instead of a sash, a rope; instead of well-dressed hair, baldness; instead of fine clothing, sackcloth; instead of beauty, branding. (vv.17–24)

The Lord took away all signs of outward beauty from these women—not because their outward beauty wasn't pleasing to Him, for it had come from Him in the first place; but because the women of Zion found their worth in outward beauty and used their beauty in ways that drew attention to themselves and away from God. And just like with the Pharisees in the New Testament, God didn't tread lightly. He made the women of Zion bald. He replaced their fine clothes with sackcloth; He took away their perfume and replaced it with stench.

I think that the most interesting part of this story can be found in verse 24. Scripture records that instead of beauty, these women would experience branding. I am sure you know that branding is the process of marking something for ownership. We are accustomed to seeing cattle being branded, and we usually wince when we see them being marked with the hot iron. Branding isn't pretty. It is a symbol of disfigurement that is the opposite of beauty. These women traded their beauty for ugly scars. I have done the same.

My beauty is God-given. So is yours. Your hair, your eyes, your skin, your figure are all gifts from God's hand. But how often do we trade in our God-given beauty for the pale imitation of beauty that comes from seeking to please the world? Or from using our beauty to draw others toward us instead of toward Christ? God is pleased by your beauty. By His creation He gives us permission to be beautiful, but His standards are clear: All beauty, both inward and outward, should point toward Him.

♡ JOURNAL PROMPTS

1. Are there times when you look fine on the outside, but your inside is a mess? How can you make sure that your outward beauty is matched by inward beauty?

2. Does the fact that the Lord isn't concerned with outward appearance make you nervous or encouraged? What beauty lies within your heart?

3. Why do you think the Lord took away the beauty of the women of Zion? What could we do to cause Him to want to strip away our beauty?

13

ROYALTY:
THE KING IS ENTHRALLED BY YOUR BEAUTY

My favorite movie is *The Princess Bride*. It is a movie filled with action, humor, suspense, and most important—romance. The lovely Buttercup falls in love with a simple farm boy named Westley. He decides he must head off to make enough money before he can marry her, but time passes and he doesn't come back. She heard that he was dead. She's heartbroken, because Westley was her only true love. She becomes betrothed to the loathsome prince of the land (against her will, of course). She is called Princess Buttercup, and her beauty becomes legendary through-out the kingdom.

Then Westley comes back, wearing a mask. She doesn't recognize him and pushes him down a hill to escape from him. As he rolls, he yells, "As . . . you . . . wish," a phrase that she heard him say often when they were back on the farm. She realizes that her beloved has come for her and flings herself down the hill after him. With danger and heroes, rescues and true love, it is a story that makes my heart flutter over and over again.

But Buttercup isn't the first princess to fascinate me. Since I was a child, the story of Cinderella escaping her life of chores to become the bride of a handsome prince has made me swoon. Whenever my chores started to pile up, I imagined a prince coming to whisk me away to a carefree life in a beautiful palace. In history class, stories of royal families always piqued my curiosity. I paid particular attention to the princesses we learned about, and allowed myself to wonder what my life would be like if I had been born into royalty. Just the other day, I watched *The Little Mermaid* again for the millionth time. Even though I knew how it ended, I still sighed with contentment when Ariel left her life as a daughter of Triton, the king of the sea, to be married to Prince Eric. I wondered if she would have made such a choice if it meant losing her status as a princess. I think the clothes and the castle would be very difficult to walk (or swim!) away from.

I bet that I am not the only one with a fascination for royalty. It seems that all little girls are enthralled by princesses and like to imagine that we could be daughters of a king and loved by a prince. We seem to be uniquely wired to desire a royal position, but why? True, princesses are beautiful, and we desire a beauty of our own to showcase. And it's true that stories about the lives of princesses are often romantic and their clothes are enough to make us drool, but is that enough to stir such a longing within us? Maybe, just maybe, we are captivated by princesses because they awaken a suspicion within us, a suspicion that there is royalty in our blood, that a crown encrusted with jewels would fit our heads perfectly, that we are princesses too.

God's Word offers us hope for these longings.

Proving Your Royal Heritage

If Christ is the King and we are His daughters, then we are indeed princesses. But with a kingdom we cannot see and a King whose face we cannot distinguish, it is easy for the power of our royal heritage to slip by us. But Scripture does not leave us to wonder. In no uncertain terms, throughout both the Old and New Testaments, Scripture confirms that we are royal heirs. The story is no less compelling than the ones we read in fairy tales, the language is no less romantic, and our beauty is no less vital.

It often happens in movies that a king dies without an heir. Typically, an evil villain stands ready to take over the throne, but just before he can, an heir is discovered. Probably the new hero doesn't look especially royal. They might have found him in an unlikely place or discovered her looking more like a peasant than a queen. But as the story unfolds, the heir's royal heritage is confirmed, the villain is vanquished, the kingdom is saved, and the townspeople celebrate.

We are the royal heirs to Christ's throne. We may not look like princesses. We probably don't know much about running kingdoms, and there is one who would seek to challenge our position as daughters of the king. But our royalty is established, and our place in the kingdom can be proven within God's Word.

Proving Christ Is a King

Christ's claim to be King is not an easy pill to swallow. We are accustomed to earthly kings. We can understand kingdoms where the boundaries are clearly defined on our maps. But Christ claims to be the King of a different kind of kingdom. It is this claim that most disturbed the religious leaders of his day.

Pilate asks Jesus about His claims to a throne. Jesus does not waver. He holds fast to His claim to the kingdom of God.

> "You *are* a king, then!" said Pilate.
> Jesus answered, . . . "You are right in saying I am a king. In fact, for this reason I was born, and for this I came into the world, to testify to the truth." (John 18:37)

Pilate misunderstood Jesus. So did many others at the time. This is why they crowned Him with a crown of thorns, wrapped Him in a scarlet robe, and mockingly bowed before Him before leading Him away to be crucified (Matthew 27:27–31). They thought He had come to establish an earthly kingdom, and when He did not they mocked and murdered Him.

But Christ is a different kind of King. His kingdom is far vaster than we can imagine, His power more complete than any other King we could ever know. First Timothy 6:15 calls Him the "King of kings" and the "Lord of lords." Revelation 1:5 establishes Him as the ruler of all of the kings of the earth. Our God is not just any king—He is the ultimate portrait of royalty.

Proving We Are Princesses

We have all watched enough Disney movies and read enough fairy tales to know that the king's children are princes and princesses. Some of them will one day inherit the throne, but all of the king's children enjoy the privileges that come with royalty. God's Word spells out the fact that we are His children and that because He has adopted us, we have inherited a royal position.

> ▶ How great is the love the Father has lavished on us, that we should be called children of God! And that is what we are! (1 John 3:1)

> ▶ In love he predestined us to be adopted as his sons through Jesus Christ, in accordance with his pleasure and will. (Ephesians 1: 4–5)

> ▶ But you are a chosen people, a royal priesthood, a holy nation, a people belonging to God, that you may declare the praises of him who called you out of darkness into his wonderful light. (1 Peter 2:9)

If our royal position were ever challenged, we could stand firm on the truth offered by God's Word that He is the King and we are His daughters. We can acknowledge with confidence that we are uniquely wired to desire a royal position and embrace our heritage as princesses.

But There's More

God doesn't just confirm our status and leave out the romance that makes fairy tales so appealing. We are not princesses who lack the beauty and splendor assigned to the king's daughters we see in movies. We too have beauty to showcase and love to rescue us.

Psalm 45 offers a portrait of the King's love for us that is so lovely and romantic and powerful that no Hollywood script could compare. These passages were written as a poem for a king, possibly King Solomon on the occasion of his wedding. But these words are also seen as a prophesy about Christ and His bride, the church. We are the princesses that the author writes about. Our beauty is the inspiration.

 Listen, O daughter, consider and give ear . . . the king is enthralled by your beauty; honor him, for he is your lord. . . . All glorious is the princess within her chamber; her gown is interwoven with gold. In embroidered garments she is led to the king; her virgin companions follow her and are brought to you. They are led in with joy and gladness; they enter the palace of the king. (vv. 10–11, 13–15)

Did you catch all of it? A king, a princess, a beautiful dress, a palace, a celebration. But did you catch the most important part, the part that announces your beauty? The part that dispels once and for all any lies that you aren't treasured, aren't valued, aren't lovely? Verse 45:11 says it plainly. "The king is enthralled by your beauty; honor him, for he is your lord."

The King is Christ and *your* beauty has enthralled Him. What does it mean to enthrall? The dictionary defines the word *enthrall* in three powerful ways. First, to enthrall means to put in bondage or to enslave. Your beauty has the power to enslave the King of kings. To enthrall also means to hold spellbound. Christ is held spellbound by your beauty, not by who you are or what you have to offer Him—though we can certainly offer gifts in these ways—but it is your beauty that holds His gaze. Finally, to enthrall means to captivate. Christ is captivated by you. He is the King. You are the princess. Your beauty holds Him transfixed.

It is hard for us to imagine this kind of romance, but we long for it, don't we? We suspect that being pursued by a king would confirm that we have worth and we are right. When the world around us seeks to sell us a version of beauty that we cannot attain, and when the people around us work to confirm that our beauty is flawed, we can rest fully in the truth that we are royalty and that the King has affirmed our worth.

What Do We Know about Princesses?

There are certain qualities that all princesses share. It is what allows us to immediately identify the princess in every story we've read about them. By studying the characteristics of princesses, we can learn a thing or two about how we are to act, now that our royal position has been secured.

Princesses Possess Beauty

Princesses are always beautiful. The story wouldn't make much sense otherwise. No prince would storm the tower for a maiden who wasn't lovely. No dragons would be fought for a princess who was flawed. If we are princesses, then we also have beauty to offer. Some of that beauty can be seen from the outside. Most of it is hidden beneath the surface. But make no mistake—you are a princess and you are beautiful.

Princesses Bear Responsibility

We expect a princess to behave a certain way and to fulfill the duties of a royal person. But what are *our* responsibilities as princesses? Specifically, what are we expected to do with our beauty?

Our first responsibility is to embrace our beauty. I am not saying that we are to parade our beauty in a way that is arrogant or immodest, but we do have a choice to continue to believe the beauty lies that others have told us or to grab hold of the truth of our beauty offered by Christ. Princesses know they are beautiful. I am sure that they have days when they struggle, when their hair and skin give them fits, but their beauty does not rest on these foundations. They are royalty. Beauty is in their blood. They know it full well.

We also have a responsibility to protect our beauty. Our beauty is a gift from the King and for the King. It is not given to us to flaunt. It is not a tool to be used to harm others. If we go back to Psalm 45:13, we see that the princess is described as glorious, but her location is protected. Her beauty is concealed within her chambers. We aren't asked to hide our beauty, but we are asked to protect it as a precious treasure.

Finally, we have a responsibility to use our beauty to point others toward the King. The princess in Psalm 45 is led to the king, and she brings others with her. First Peter 2:9 tells us that we have been declared as royalty so that we can announce God's praises. Ultimately, all of the beauty we have to offer, both our inner and outer beauty, is to be used to draw attention toward our Father, not toward us.

Princesses Are Worth Fighting For

A fairy tale would be dry without a battle to be fought. Westley conquered giants and swordsmen and crossed seas and swamps to rescue Princess Buttercup. Prince Charming searched far and wide for his princess, armed only with her glass slipper. Prince Eric fought the Sea Witch to win Ariel's hand. As princesses, we long for our princes to ride to our rescue.

And if Christ is our Savior, we are rescued indeed. Dwell on what He has done and will do:

> ▶ He brought me out into a spacious place; he rescued me because he delighted in me. (Psalm 18:19)

- Grace and peace to you from God our Father and the Lord Jesus Christ, who gave himself for our sins to rescue us from the present evil age, according to the will of our God and Father. (Galatians 1:3–4)

- For he has rescued us from the dominion of darkness and brought us into the kingdom of the Son he loves. (Colossians 1:13)

- The Lord will rescue me from every evil attack and will bring me safely to his heavenly kingdom. (2 Timothy 4:18)

You are worth fighting for. Christ has slain the dragon and defeated the foe, and He has done it all out of His love for you. You are His princess and you are worth fighting for. Earthly princes may not see it. They may not fight for you, but it does not mean that your worth is shaky. Your beauty compels Him and He will fight for you. He stands ready to rescue you over and over again.

Princesses Are Adored by the King

Sometimes in real life, fathers dismiss or ignore their daughters. But this is not the stuff of fairy tales. In stories and in movies, the king almost always adores his daughter. He seeks out her best interest. He pours out his praise for her. Sometimes he offers expensive gifts as signs of his affection. A true princess is obviously adored by the king.

You are adored by your King. He loves you. His love does not change. He will fight for you. His resolve does not waver. He is enthralled by you. Your beauty holds Him spellbound.

I don't know who else adores you. I don't know who else is telling you that you are beautiful. I don't know who else has the courage to confirm your worth. But I know that you are adored. I know that you are beautiful. I know that you are worth dying for. This is the foundation on which you can build your sense of yourself. God sees your beauty and your value. Can you see it too?

"The king is enthralled by your beauty; honor him, for he is your lord" (Psalm 45:11).

♡ JOURNAL PROMPTS

1. Which fairy tales were your favorites when you were a little girl? Why did you love these stories?

2. Is it difficult for you to imagine that Christ seeks to romance you the way the king romances the princess in Psalm 45:11? How do you feel about the fact that He is enthralled by your beauty?

3. In what ways has God rescued you? In what areas of your life do you still need to be rescued?

4. Can you see your beauty? Can you embrace the value that God's Word assigns to you?

5. How does this change the way that you feel about yourself?

GLANCING IN THE REARVIEW MIRROR:
A LOOK BACK AT THE JOURNEY

EPILOGUE

 I wish I could say that the battle is won, that my sword is on display in a glass case because I know that I will never again have to draw it against the urge to see myself as something other than Christ's beautiful, treasured child. As I deliver this message to others I wish I could say, "Look at me. I *used to* struggle with body image, but those days are gone. I no longer try to fit the mold of culture, no longer listen to the whisperings of the Evil One."

But that is not the case. Bad days still come. Tears still flow on occasion because I fall into old habits and buy old lies. But victory will come through dependence on Jesus, and there is undeniable power in knowing that I am His creation, fearfully and wonderfully made in His image.

There is also power in the encouragement of others, girls just like you who take the time to give compliments, hold me accountable, and share similar frustrations. I know that Christ will continue to hold me on His anvil and continue to shape me into the woman He wants me to be. I know that He will do the same for you. I want you to know that I am praying for you, praying that you will continue to depend on Jesus in all areas of struggle, praying that you will get a glimpse of your worth in Christ, and praying that you will learn to see the art in yourself.

Thank you for taking this journey with me.

NOTES

CHAPTER 2: THE HISTORY OF BEAUTY

1. Drea Leed, "Elizabethan Makeup 101," July–August 2001, http://www.rencentral.com/jul_aug_vol1/makeup101.shtml.

2. Jane H. Marchduk, "History of Lipstick," http://www.helium.com/items/862230-watch-history-lipstickwhat-would.

3. Jimmy Dunn, "Facial Hair (specifically beards) in Ancient Eqypt," http://www.touregypt.net/featurestories/beards.htm.

4. Joan Styan, "Wartime Hardships: Rationing in London," http://www.bbc.co.uk/ww2peopleswar/stories/98/a2756298.shtml, (2004).

5. Lydia Boyd, "Brief History of Beauty and Hygiene Products," http://scriptorium.lib.duke.edu/adaccess/cosmetics-history.html.

6. Christy Tillery French, "The History of Makeup," October 2, 2004, http://www.authorsden.com/visit/viewArticle.asp?id=15438.

7. James A. Crites, "Chinese Foot Binding," October 25, 1995, http://www.angelfire.com/ca/beekeeper/foot.html.

8. G. Gaesser, *Big Fat Lies: The Truth about Your Weight and Health* (New York: Fawcett Columbine, 1996).

9. Margo Maine, *Body Wars: Making Peace with Women's Bodies* (Carlsbad, Cal.: Gurze Books, 2000), 192.

10. K. D. Brownell and J. Rodin, "The Dieting Maelstrom," *American Psychologist,* 49(9): 781–791.

11. H. W. Hoek and D. van Hoeken, "Review of the Prevalence and Incidence of Eating Disorders," *International Journal of Eating Disorders* (2003): 383–396.

12. Sam Levenson, *In One Era and Out the Other* (New York: Simon & Schuster, 1973), 177.

CHAPTER 3: WALKING ON BROKEN GLASS

1. George L. Kelling and James Q. Wilson, "Broken Windows," *Atlantic Monthly* (March 1982).

CHAPTER 4: LAYING THE FOUNDATION

1. Sharon Hersh, *Mom, I Feel Fat!* (Colorado Springs: WaterBrook, 2001), 66–70.

CHAPTER 5: WHERE DO THESE FEELINGS COME FROM?

1. Reader's comments, name withheld, *Self* (October 2006), 28.

2. Debra Waterhouse, *Like Mother; Like Daughter* (New York: Hyperion, 1997), 15.

3. J. K. Rowling, http://www.jkrowling.com (biography).

CHAPTER 6: MIXED MESSAGES

1. Emily A. Hamilton, Lauri Mintz, and Susan Kashubeck-West, "Predictors of Media Effects on Body Dissatisfaction in European American Women," *Sex Roles: A Journal of Research,* vol. 56, nos. 5–6, (March 2007): 397–402.

2. Jean Kilbourne, "Beauty . . . and the Beast of Advertising," http://www.medialit.org/reading_room/article40.html.

3. Walt Mueller, "Getting Taken: What You and Your Teens Need to Know about Marketing (Part 1)," http://www.cpyu.org/Page.aspx?id=275909.

4. Ron Harris, "Children Who Dress for Excess: Today's Youngsters Have Become Fixated with Fashion. The Right Look Isn't Enough—It Also Has to Be Expensive," *Los Angeles Times* (November 12, 1989).

5. Jeff Schewe, "Kate Doesn't Like Photoshop—Digital Ethics," *Photoshop News,* http://photoshopnews.com/2005/04/03/kate-doesn't-like-photoshop.

6. Walt Mueller, Ibid.

CHAPTER 7: IMPERFECT? JOIN THE CROWD

1. Kendall Payne and Kara Powell, *Mirror, Mirror* (Grand Rapids: Zondervan/Youth Specialties, 2003), 69.

CHAPTER 8: BUT WHY CAN'T I LOOK LIKE SHE DOES?

1. Phillip C. McGraw, *O, The Oprah Magazine,* April 1, 2006.

2. Ibid.

CHAPTER 9: THE TROUBLE WITH BODY IMAGE

1. David Garner, "Survey Says: Body Image Poll Results," *Psychology Today* (January/February 1997), 30.

2. "Teen Girls on a Diet More Likely to Smoke," http://www.msnbc.msn.com/id/20759963/.

3. "Did You Know . . . ," http://womentodaymagazine.com/fitnesshealth/bodyimage.html.

4. This information comes from the National Eating Disorders Association Web site. The site listing is http://www.nationaleatingdisorders.org/p.asp?WebPage_ID=286&Profile_ID=41157.

5. Aaron Levin, "Teens' Distorted Body Image May Lead to Unhealthy Behaviors," July 16, 2003, http://www.cfah.org/hbns/news/distort07-16-03.cfm.

CHAPTER 10: DISORDERED EATING

1. J. H. Crowther, E. M. Wolf, and N. Sherwood, *The Etiology of Bulimia Nervosa: The Individual and Familial Context* (Washington, D.C.: Taylor & Francis, 1992), 1–26.

2. H. W. Hoek and D. van Hoeken "Review of the Prevalence and Incidence of Eating Disorders," *International Journal of Eating Disorders* 34 (2003): 383–396.

3. National Eating Disorders Association, 2006, www.nationaleating disorders.org.

4. C. M. Shisslak, M. Crago, and L. S. Estes, "The Spectrum of Eating Disturbances," *International Journal of Eating Disorders* (1995): 209–219.

5. D. Neumark-Sztainer, *I'm, Like, SO Fat!* (New York: Guilford Press, 2005), 5.

CHAPTER 13: GOD'S VIEW OF BEAUTY

1. John and Stasi Eldredge, *Captivating* (Nashville: Thomas Nelson, 2005), 40.

ISBN-10: 0-8024-4585-3
ISBN-13: 978-0-8024-4585-8

ISBN-10: 0-8024-4586-5
ISBN-13: 978-0-8024-4586-5

Our culture is driven by a concept of beauty that negatively impacts adolescent girls. The Scriptures are full of assurances regarding our identity in Christ, inherent worth to the Creator, and the secrets to tapping into the source of true and lasting beauty, yet girls and young women continue to struggle with their focus on outer beauty. In *Graffiti: Learning to See the Art in Ourselves*, Erin Davis applies the language of God's Word on identity, beauty, and worth to the life of a contemporary young woman. In fact, women who have never adequately dealt with this issue will find themselves reviewing their youth, and redirecting their spiritual eyes. Don't miss the *Leader's Guide*, which provides small group leaders with ideas for retreat activities and going deeper.

by Erin Davis

Find it now at your favorite local or online bookstore.

www.MoodyPublishers.com